Facedown on the pavement, my head cushioned in my arms against the blast, in the position of grief, I waited. My body yearned toward the protection of the concrete. It would not let me in. The air split apart in a vast yell of sound. The pavement surged up to slap my chest.

Then there was silence, and through me, in answer to the slap, a surge of life that had halted in the waiting. I was alive, vulnerable on the pavement. I got up. I walked on. Behind me the sounds of rescue turned into a mews. I smelled the arid flying rubble of the burst houses, but I did not look back. We did not gape at the death of other people. There was a politeness.

I picked up a hot piece of shrapnel with my hankerchief. I was in the relief of life. After such recognitions, to be alive is to bear a gift, a sense of gentleness, never a right. Through the war one felt it given, over and over, as a gift.

ALL THE BRAVE PROMISES

Memories of Aircraft Woman
2nd Class 2146391

Mary Lee Settle

BALLANTINE BOOKS • NEW YORK

*To the wartime other ranks of the
Women's Auxiliary Air Force, Royal
Air Force—below the rank of sergeant*

Library of Congress Catalog Card Number: 66-13651

ISBN 0-345-28660-X

This edition published by arrangement with Delacorte Press

Manufactured in the United States of America

First Ballantine Books Edition: November 1980

Recall

We are accused of being nostalgic. We have been. What we have remembered are events. The Second World War was, for most of us, a state, a state of war, not an event. It was a permeation, a deadening, a waiting, hard to recall. What we have told about is the terrifying relief of battle or the sweet, false relief of leave.

These were not the causes of a psychic shock from which a generation of people are only now beginning to emerge. For every "historic" event, there were thousands of unknown, plodding people, caught up in a deadening authority, learning to survive by keeping quiet, by "getting by," by existing in secret, underground; conscripted, shunted, numbered. It took so many of them, so many of their gray days and their uprooted lives. It taught them evasive ways to survive. These ways, dangerous to the community and to the spirit, have been a part of the peace.

It is one small corner of this wartime life—the part of the Women's Auxiliary Air Force of the Royal Air Force in England—that I want to recall, perhaps to explain, to find out about, as I did then, step by step.

Having long since learned the lesson of "no names, no pack drill," both names and places have been "scrambled."

Chapter 1

By January, 1942, all women in Britain over the age of eighteen and under the age of sixty were conscripted either for factories, essential jobs and nursing or for the Armed Forces. Those of us who volunteered for the Forces were either seventeen, or Irish, or colonials, or romantics like myself who could persuade an official to let them aboard a ship.

I began trying to volunteer in Washington. In that hot summer of 1942, the diplomats and the Allied officers and the new American soldiers on leave shared taxis and talked about the war abstractly in the crowded cocktail bars or at parties on the tiny lawns in Georgetown. We saw *Mrs. Miniver* and *In Which We Serve*. Lludmilla Pavlechenka, the Russian sniper, short, square, with a heavy, boy's body and a child's face who was said to have killed five hundred Germans, sat in a box at an all-Russian concert. She wore a thick brown-blanket uniform with a tight red collar in the sweltering heat of the Washington summer. Her cheeks were painted in round, red patches like Petrouchka's. She watched us, crowded below her, as we filed into the concert hall, thin and cool in our summer evening dresses, to honor her. Whenever Russians came to the diplomatic parties, always in the background stood two officers looking exactly alike, saying nothing, only watching, with the highest polish on their boots in Washington. They were known as Tweedledum and Tweedledee.

There were little, isolated pockets of people who had been to the war. I shared a house with four code-and-cypher officers of the Women's Auxiliary Air Force of the Royal Air Force. On the hot nights, sweltering in new American underwear, they talked about Biggin Hill and the Battle of Britain. One had seen her husband killed, gone back to Canada to have her child, left the baby with her parents and come back to the WAAF. They took my attempts to join up for granted. In their atmosphere such decisions seemed normal.

Then there was a sense of war among the Allied officers, meeting at parties, sustained by the control of their manners, strolling at night under the trees, bright with light, sitting on the steps of the Lincoln Memorial—I remember all these times, constantly talking about war, and then I remembered St. Petersburg in *War and Peace,* where manners were important and gestures meant more than their action, and war was someplace else. It was what I would learn to call officer's war, with its new sense of elegance and its place for so many, its oases of comfort and dash so many would miss, forgetting or suppressing or never experiencing the rest.

At the British Embassy, the assistant military attaché, the assistant air attaché and the assistant naval attaché (they were all very tall and thin in their meticulous summer uniforms) discussed my case. They rejected me for the WRENS because I might be posted to Cairo, and the white, cotton summer stockings of their uniforms would hide my legs. They decided that in the Women's Army (the ATS) I would have no one to talk to. Then they set the unwieldy machinery of government going, almost casually, so that I could join the WAAF.

I was put aboard the train in Washington with a last bottle of champagne and an armful of roses. In my trunk were a year's supply of toilet paper, can after can of fruit juice, and evening clothes. I left what for nearly three years I would look back on as the last prewar world—a cloud cuckoo land, exciting and full of luxury.

The *City of Delhi* lay in dock at a pier near the bottom of Manhattan. At night, when I first looked up at her from the dock, she loomed above me, a dimmed-out ghost ship, the first lowering of lights toward Europe, out of place in New York, where the dimout of the docks hardly reached the bright streets. In peace-time she plied between Port Said and Calcutta. She still had Lashkar hands, and her louvered cabin doors had let in the still air of the Indian Ocean. This was in September, hot at night in New York.

There was a tension aboard the ship I could not name—not yet. She was loaded more quietly than ships are loaded in peacetime. At each door were two black-out curtains. We were instructed to let the first one drop, stand between them until we could see no light, then open the outer one to go on deck at night. We were told how far a cigarette glow or the lighting of a match showed across the Atlantic water. The portholes were screwed down, their heavy iron storm shutters im-movable.

At the late supper, served in dock, the Norwegian first mate of a tanker torpedoed in the Caribbean told me not to carry my Mae West life jacket. He said that where we were going the water was too cold to live in for more than ten minutes. We ate curry that first night—and every night after—as if the ship, like the people aboard her, were holding on to some peacetime identity against the impersonal state of war.

In the morning, on deck, there was a sense of holi-day. A British air attaché and his tall wife strode twenty times around the deck, solemnly walking their mile of exercise. As they walked they looked at us all as if they were choosing candy from a box. Later they sin-gled me out to have pink gin with them in the tiny bar, opened an hour a day. I was carefully instructed on who it was possible to speak to—sadly few—aboard the ship.

We slipped on toward the convoy rendezvous off Nova Scotia through a dim, muting offshore mist.

Groups of passengers sat around the deck, still cling-ing to those they knew—a few civilians like myself, a group of torpedoed survivors from merchant ships in the Caribbean, watchful, some still showing wounds, all returning to take ships again from England; a flight of navigators of the Fleet Air Arm, returning to be posted to ships after training, all but one of them to be commissioned as midshipmen. They were seventeen, too young to be lieutenants. Mothers who had been evacuated to the British islands in the Caribbean with their children, too homesick to stay among strangers out of danger, plucked at their children's collars to keep them quiet and stared at the misty water. There were seventy-five passengers on the *City of Delhi,* sister ship to the *City of Benares,* which had been torpedoed two years before with a shipload of children with their mothers, going out to the same safety these women were leaving.

The flight of navigators, in their bell-bottomed trousers and blouses of the English Navy, began to sing, "There are gallons of paint on Orion's shipside, and Jimmy looks on them with pride." A few of the mothers moved their children around the deck, afraid the song would have dirty words.

Later, in the pitch-black night, the louvered doors creaked and the ship groaned and breathed as she slowed and turned. Under the dim lights of the small lounge—furnished, like an English suburban parlor, with faded chintz and fringed lamps and magazine racks with old torn copies of *Punch* and the *Tatler* flopping over the worn wooden bars—we sat around on chairs and the floor. Derek, a pale, childlike boy looking, in his "sailor suit," as if he should be carrying a toy boat to the park, had drunk a little too much of the warm pink gin. He kept his eyes averted from the slightly swaying fringe of the lamps. He was holding on to the arm of a battened-down chair as if his small, unballasted body wanted to carry his angel face out on the deck to be sick and he had to resist it.

He told me that he had thought he was going to be a priest as if it were not his own choice but was a foregone decision beyond himself that he be sent as an apprentice of God. With some surprise he asked me if I thought God minded when he joined up "to do as the others did." Then he added, "I only allowed myself one luxury, though. I thought that if I had to die, I would rather it be in the air. I'm jolly bad at dirt."

One of the other midshipmen noticed his pale face and called a cure for seasickness across the lounge, "Swallow a cold pork chop with a string, then pull it up again, Derek."

Derek ran, clawing at the blackout curtain. As he disappeared, the same midshipman called out, "Don't panic. Remember, you're British" and laughed.

A little apart, watching us but not speaking until he was spoken to, a thin boy in the outgrown uniform of an apprentice in the merchant navy sat very tall in his chair. His wrists stood out beyond his jacket sleeves, and the heavy socks someone had knitted for him were a wide expanse between his trouser cuffs and his worn shoes, brightly polished. His thatch of red hair had risen out of the confinement of his cap like a halo when he came into the lounge, bending his head by habit as if all doors made were too low for him. He sat straight, holding the cap in his lap, waiting. From the left side of his hairline, across his forehead, through his right eyebrow and down to his right ear, a deep livid scar ran in a clean straight line, vicious and ludicrous on his schoolboy face. Finally, someone asked him what his name was.

He said, "It's Lofty," in a soft, highland Scot's accent. He went on sitting there, a long ungainly bird among the flight of navigators, as close in movement as a flight of night-blue pigeons.

Later in the night I watched the ocean, musty dark against a softer dark sky. After a time I could see the high aftermast of the freighter, vague against the darkness like an empty crucifix, swaying in time with the ship's turning. We seemed to be isolated in black space. Someone was standing a little apart from me. I could hear him cough, once.

When he spoke, I knew it was Lofty.

Out of the darkness his voice came, low, as if he were listening beyond it, "I don't know what you're doing here."

Out of darkness I answered, "I'm going to join up."

There was a long silence. The ship's rigging creaked and sighed.

"This is no' the war. Ach, it's a rest. Wait 'til you see in the morning."

When I left the deck, he was still standing on a kind of watch of his own.

I think excitement rolled through the ship and woke us all at dawn. When I got on deck, the passengers were lined along the rails, their British groups broken for once, staring and pointing out to sea.

The convoy spread out around us over the gray water, a vast formal checkerboard of ships—some so far away that they seemed like toys—in the geometric pattern that I would always remember as a part of the war: the man-imposed square designs on the undisciplined elements of earth or air or water. There were a hundred ships in the convoy, but in the vast surrounding space they must have looked from the air or to the undersea questors as tiny and illusive as a flotilla of leaves.

Behind me, Lofty said, "You see. We're in the safe center of the convoy. I could tell by the ship's complement."

He pointed to the "coffin corners" almost out of sight at the corners of the huge square. These were the ships in most danger of being picked off by marauding U-boats. I was told that if they were hit, no one stopped to pick up survivors—the German U-boats waited for rescue ships and sank them. I began to feel the reality of the Norwegian first mate's advice not to prolong the time in the water with a Mae West. We cruised along at four knots.

In and out along the aisles between the ships, two Canadian corvettes, our escort, moved around us, long, thin white pencils in the water.

It grew, as we sailed slowly that morning, grew to a level of recognition and stayed with us—fear, rolling along under us like an imagined double, an evil alter ego to our sailing. No one mentioned it except quietly to another single person or in jokes or in sudden silences that followed unfamiliar sounds.

For the rest, we were young and we were at sea, and fear became a pitch of excitement, of pranks or entertainment. We poured gin in the water jugs to drink when the bar was closed. We sang the same songs over and over. We burst into the lounge in the evenings to listen to the one member of the flight over seventeen, an ex-CID officer. We made him our father and sat on the floor around him. He told stories of the Black Museum at Scotland Yard, and we listened with the comfort of hearing something familiar to scare us, while the air attaché and his wife gathered up their magazines and made a disapproving British exit.

All the time, we were sailing north by northeast.

The North Atlantic ocean has its own color and its own seasons, perpetually changing; yet all over, in memory, a great plain, slowly breathing, which slopes toward America turning green and toward the coast of England, a cold blue, almost black, studded with stern ecclesiastical white, while in between, we sailed on through weeks of gray ocean time; there was no sensation of space traveled so slowly, only of time and an almost imperceptible change of color; no directional movement, only the horizon's sinking and soaring as we rode the steep troughs and high hills of the ocean.

Lofty had made himself my guide. He must have sensed that I felt like an ungainly bird, too, out of my element of comfort and protection, feeling more and more, every day, the cold exposure of a decision made, a decision that was no longer a caprice to shrug away, no longer a possible, easy change of mind, but was an inevitable four-knot journey to war. I was beginning to recognize its state, the waiting, the watchfulness against an unknown, unseen abstract called Jerry—the enemy—a state under consciousness of slow, energy-sucking awareness. Besides all that, the others pretended to have trouble understanding us both, me a Southerner, and he from north of Aberdeen.

We had been at sea for two weeks when I thought I

was awakened by a faraway sound in the night, but I can't be sure; perhaps it was only dreaming, perhaps retrospect.

In the early morning Lofty showed me the right rear coffin corner. It was empty. I could see the other ships changing places on the horizon. By noon the corner was closed. It seemed as abstract as losing a pawn in chess. Most of the men keeping a kind of vigil along the starboard rail that morning were the merchant seamen. They said little, only watched while the convoy reclosed its square.

In the early afternoon the claxon alarm sounded through the still, waiting sea air. There were watery booms in the distance from the corvettes, great fans of spray; then, over the side of our own ship was launched, from a slow catapult, what looked like an enormous beer barrel rolling toward the water. The depth charge disappeared under the slate-gray sea; its surface swelled up and up above undersea sound and burst in a great jet of white spume. We were not attacked again; whatever marauder had lurked along after us was gone or sunk, and the water had closed back over where it had been as impersonally as the ship in the early morning had neatly sailed to close the convoy's coffin corner.

Years later I read in Churchill's book *The Hinge of Fate* that October, 1942, had been a climactic month in the Battle of the Atlantic. Nothing of this was spoken aboard ship, but I was later to look at the map of convoys' sinkings, with those neat dots that mean statistics of death, and I realized that during that week we must have entered the center strip of the Atlantic, out of range of coastal planes from either side. So war seemed to be fought on plans instead of actuality, for on the American side of the ocean we never saw a plane.

We had been at sea two weeks. Now an event had heightened our awareness; the ship itself was permeated with new watchfulness, as if she had a hunted soul. That night, noisy with a new surge of excitement, we planned a show. I would see this happen over and over, when the event, the battle, no matter how terrible, would break the debilitating stalemate of the body in its state of war and cause a communal adrenalin rise—a precious, simple sense of being vulnerable and alive. In convoy, it was the exposure of the slow majestic duck before the quick, sly mink.

So we entertained, rehearsing as carefully as if we were going on at the Palladium as soon as we landed. I had never seen the English en masse before, and my first and always-with-me memory is of them in the gallery; tables pushed back to the wall, an improvised stage and faces, guileless with pleasure, warmed in the pale light. The women, the children, the merchant seamen—even the air attaché and his wife—sang, mouths open, as trusting as fledglings, led by a Yorkshire boy in bell-bottomed trousers, his little stocky figure tight girdled in his Navy blouse, who was bawling out a lusty "On Ilkly Morr Ba Taat."

Why do charades, with the sly digs at authority the British seem born with, seem so vulnerable in their pleasure that they leave a lump in the throat?

The climax, "Old Folks, Young Folks," raised the roof. Even Lofty jumped up and, leaning forward like a stork, belted out in his almost-unintelligible accent,

> "Tha King said to Salome,
> We'll hae no dancin' here.
> Salome said to hale wi' ye
> And kicked the chandelier."

Afterwards, under an illusive white moon, breaking from time to time through the darker clouds in the dark sky, Lofty and I walked slowly around the blacked-out deck, used by now to the dark, aware by a new sense, so well developed in the blind, of the bulkheads, the stanchions, the other isolated human figures. From time to time the moon cast the shadow of the mast along the deck, and I knew that the telltale shadow of our ships would be cast across the black swell of the ocean's surface. It was bitter cold.

Seeping into my ken was a new thing. I was learning to live with fear—not a caught breath warning danger, as of a fall, but a presence—a patient, lasting undertone, an evil possibility. To look back on safety was to look back on a kind of physical innocence, an unknowing never to be regained. Gray was its color—all the fog-gray, sea-gray, gray of rubble, of endless English days, like the inside of a brain, gray in faces, especially of women, gray joyless sex, tired gray dirty arms, fatigue-gray. All other color I remember is in contrast to this basic dim twilight gray of the war.

I have to read again the sparkling, frenetic speeches of Churchill and of Roosevelt, and I have lost much of the ambiance of the few great events, but I can call back the gray silent fear of the war, as if it waited forever in my skull, and Lofty's strange, soft, confiding *brrrh* of a voice that night as, protected by darkness, he held my hand carefully to guide me along the deck. From time to time the moon lit his face, and the scar made it look like a photograph, torn across.

He said, "You're a poor fool to be doing this."

I thought of my send-off at the station in Washington—the roses, the champagne, the inevitable "new beige suit" for traveling. Now I wore a quilted Clarkson suit, borrowed from one of the Fleet Air Arm navigators, against the icy wind.

Lofty said, "You know nothing about it. I've read the Yank papers. They make it sound like one of your Yank flicks."

I said nothing.

He went on softly, "I'll tell you what I've not told before. I won't survive it. I'm caught in it. We're all caught up in it. You people ask for it. All that heroics. It's bloody dangerous."

"Didn't *you* volunteer?" I asked him.

"Aye, when I was fourteen. Three years ago this September. But it's no' the same for a mon."

Near us the moon slid out from behind the dark clouds; one figure parted and became two. It was the Norwegian first mate and one of the returning mothers.

When we had walked out of earshot up into the bow, rising and falling among the few stars on the horizon, Lofty stopped and said, "There's a thing like a great beast in the water. It's following me. It's not even a Jerry—just a great beast like my Weird. It's found me twice. Once, in the North Sea, I was picked up by a Norwegian trawling for herring. Aye, I'm sick of eating bloody herring. I like the curry better. You get a taste for it."

A star fell and disappeared behind the water.

"The second time, I got caught by the ship's prop in the Caribbean. We were one day out of Trinidad. I spent two months in a hospital in Trinidad. Lovely sun. The music's a bit heathen for my taste.

"Next time it will get me."

I wondered how much he'd missed, and I wanted to tease him, because he was too near the truth, too Celtic in his foretelling of the beast in my own mind.

I said, "Lofty, have you ever been in love?"

"Aye, once," he said. "She sat in front of me in an eight-oar rowboat. We were crossing one of the great fjords—mostly refugees and a few British sailors. The Norwegian fishermen were taking us to where we could get out of Norway. The civilians were going north, not to anyplace, just away from the Jerrys. She had long blond hair in pleats, and a little face. Her eyes were blue."

"Did you speak to her?"

"No. We could no' speak the language. We watched each other all the way across the fjord."

"What did you do?"

"I just pleated and unpleated her hair."

A week out of England a small cheer went up through the hollow sea wind. Someone pointed out a Sunderland Flying Boat of the RAF Coastal Command. It dipped its wings gull-like and flew out of sight. But we sensed protection and began to watch for land.

We sailed north of Ireland. The corvettes darted in and out between the ships, and the sailors waved. The convoy began to take on a playful atmosphere, gay as a school of dolphins, in the strongly patrolled coastal waters, after a month at sea. A few wide-ranging gulls circled the rigging, their harsh calling a comfort, and disappeared toward the land.

One morning the sea around us was empty. The convoy had dispersed during the night. We sailed on alone. At twilight, about three in the afternoon so far north, we sighted the Hebrides—magnificent hills of pink and purple rock rising out of the water, lit by the wan setting sun, the first sight of Europe, stripped to rock, beautiful and bare.

Lofty told us all they were the Hebrides, then told us again, full of pride.

In the dawn, the next day or the next, time lost, we slipped down through the Irish Sea along a corridor of fog, feeling the way silently. From the bow, the stern was a creeping ghost in ghost air. We lined the railings to peer down through the mist to see the pilot boat loom alongside, as if it had materialized in mist, had not come from anywhere.

On the Mersey River the fog had lifted a foot or so above the water, so we could see no land, only the oily dirty surface of the river mouth and in it, into the distance, a vast cemetery of ships, only their masts or their funnels showing just above the water to mark their graves. All around us, breaking the silence of the fog, the unseen gulls shrieked, sometimes diving into sight to rest on the oily surface among the masts, then taking off again, becoming invisible, screaming.

Gradually the fog lifted. We were moored at one of the wide wooden floating docks undulating in the tidal river.

The center of Liverpool looked as if some vast filthy foot had trampled it, not noticing that it was a city. I started to say "inhuman," but only humans could do such fouling of a nest. Around the flattened middle, the ruins jutted up bedraggled, unkempt and neglected as rotten teeth.

There were no crowds at the dock. Only a few longshoremen wandered down to the ship. In the distance I could see people walking in the flattened square. They looked dreamlike in the last of the mist. One of the longshoremen, a garrulous old man, pointed out with pride that high above the city, the statue of the liver bird on the still-standing Royal Liver Building soared under the risen fog. As we landed I noticed a new smell after the clean sea: dust, war dust compounded of rubble, old smoke traces, neglect and fatigue, and with it the sad smell I could not place—smoke from chimneys of the impure wartime coal, a whiff of formaldehyde, reminding me of specimen butterflies caught on pins.

The boat train stood in the dockside. In all the mess, it looked as healthy and busy as when the napkin wiped Charlie Chaplin's mouth after the breakdown of the machine in *Modern Times*.

The English countryside dripped, sleepy and vague, in the misty rain. The midshipmen talked about getting their officer's uniforms at last, and people ran back and forth along the corridor of the train, trying to beat life back into sea friendships already waning on the land. I promised Lofty and one of the midshipmen that I would meet them at the Berkeley bar in three days if I had not already been sent into the WAAF.

An officer from the Ministry of Labor put his head into the carriage, checking the recruits. A dim-looking man, with his trench coat, small moustache, carefully combed sparse hair and prewar attaché case full of overhandled-looking papers, he was the first of so many I would see—be shunted by—through the war. They were a type, and they reminded me of brown bedrooms in boarding houses in Pimlico where separate thick sugar bowls carried their painted names. They were what the British called ex-officer types, made of strong tea, beer, too little sex, too many buns, cheap conservative socks, cracking, carefully polished shoes.

I was told that we would be taken to billets in London.

He consulted a paper and gave me a date to report for my medical examination at the WAAF recruiting center in Kingsway.

He said "we," but when the train reached London, I was the only recruit. The few others had managed to call from Liverpool, and they were met by little knots of people in the huge St. Pancras station. He drove me by taxi to the St. Pancras Veterinary Hospital, which was to be my billet until I went into the WAAF. I was signed in to some vague shape of a woman there. When you become a package for delivery, all shapes become vague. She took me to my bed.

It was in a long, high room, probably used to parade sick animals in peacetime, for it had a sick-animal smell—or was that only the first scent of anonymity? There must have been fifty cots lined along the walls. She told me the rest were used by Irish laborers being recruited by "the Ministry." What ministry she didn't say, only that they were a sorry lot, and "up all hours."

War was one thing. St. Pancras Veterinary Hospital was another. I had not yet learned not to step backward.

I put my toothbrush in my handbag and a nightgown in my pocket and went out into the deadening twilight, that strange twilight where no lights went up in warm windows to show that evening had begun. There was only a gradual flattening out, a loss of perspective in the streets, disappearing in the blacked-out darkness. Down the long street of solid houses, I could see a tear in the roofscape, a missing house, neatly plucked out, now cleaned in 1942 so that it had the terrible innocence of a doll's house; the front was gone, showing a rained-on piece of wallpaper in an upstairs room, an untouched second-floor fireplace hanging in mid-air, a stairway that went nowhere. I saw a taxi, its slatted blackout lights almost obliterated in the deep dusk.

Since the Ritz, the Savoy, the Berkeley and Claridge's were the only hotels I had heard of in London, I told the taxi driver Claridge's. I knew the others would be expensive, and I had come to England with a hundred dollars.

When the taxi drew up in Davies Street and I was fumbling with the new, strange money, the door was opened and a voice said, "Good evening, Madame." I looked up into the eyes of a tall, red man, in a shiny top hat. A small voice inside me said a punched-in-the-stomach "oh."

When I presented myself to the receptionist and explained that my suitcases were at the St. Pancras Veterinary Hospital, he simply took out a key and said to the porter, "Show Madame to her room." For that straight face and that aloof kindness, I would be grateful always.

By the next day, war had reassumed something of its Washington air—rescue by friends, lunch, a promise of the country, that suffused glow they gave me of an act, amusing, but well done. So when, three days later, I told a friend from the Foreign Office that I had two midshipmen to meet at the Berkeley bar, he wanted to come along, to see who I'd traveled with.

We had been sitting at one of the tables for a few minutes when Derek, creaking in his new uniform, appeared at the door. He sat on the edge of a small chair, his cap in his hand as if, having earned it, he didn't want to give it up. The waiter whispered, the diplomat left the table and came back. Derek, Fleet Air Arm navigator, midshipman, was underage to be served alcohol. In a minute two more midshipmen arrived, then three more. The silent circle enlarged around the little table; two more pulled up chairs, schoolboy polite in what they called "a posh hotel." In half an hour there was a circle like a seance spread over the center of the bar. Twenty-four navigators and Lofty, taller, more awkward than the rest, his scar almost blue against his blushing face, sat with the table afloat in the middle to drink ginger beer and say good-bye.

A year later I met one of them in a street in London. He said that all but four of the rest were dead.

Chapter 2

The London of that week, as I waited to go into the WAAF, was "really" there as I had hoped, part of a language I already knew, as a memory before an event. I could still impose what I expected, comfortably, on what I saw, and it was life going on with a clung-to stability I took as normal, except for cleaned-up, neat gaps in its roofscapes, diminished against the solidity of its buildings—what was missing was less surprising than what was still there.

I lunched with a friend at Madame Prunier's in St. James's Street on the day I was to report. It had, that day, the intimacy against the cold space of October that London restaurants seem designed for, a cozy, good-smelling womb of adulthood, sweet from the pastry, a discreet tingle of glass and silver, polite murmurings, crowded but still quiet. It was a farewell lunch—small slices of good cake, Boeuf à la Bourguignonne and a rare bottle of prewar rosé from Anjou. When the bill came, my friend suggested that she pay for the food and I pay for the wine.

I walked out of Prunier's, small suitcase in hand, dressed carefully (so as not to "stand out"—this was instinctive) in an old camel's hair coat, a heavy Harris tweed suit, Pinet shoes and equipped with two hundred Balkan Sobranie cigarettes I had been given as a present and exactly one shilling. I stood staring across the road at officers' caps in Lock's, wondering how to walk to Kingsway—mapping it in my mind, damp London cold soaking through my heavy clothes. At that second a surge toward the unknown swept over me, a feeling of freedom, of guy ropes released, that can only be had once. It is an illusion that the past can be cast away so easily, as if one had only to let go for it to disappear; but, in action, that day freedom seemed pure. The feel-

ing, and the wine, the excitement, the cold as off the
end of a springboard, made me gasp, in that second, for
breath.

So, light as air, I swung past St. James's Palace, sunk-
en and small at the end of the street, and into the
Mall, where across the wide, nearly deserted esplande
beyond its bordering trees St. James's Park lay veiled in
the gray-green of October, air and trees almost translu-
cent under the pale sun. Above me to my left, the elegant Regency façade of Carlton House terrace was neglected looking, disheveled by piles of sandbags soaked
in damp. At the Admiralty, the huge, squat, angled
monolith of a wartime building looked like it had been
left from a barbarian time long before the rise of the
Admiralty Arch or the delicate structure of the Horse
Palace in the distance behind it.

Past the few people crisscrossing Trafalgar Square,
where, in the distance, antlike dark figures in their wartime drab were strung out thinly in a late queue for the
canteen below the National Gallery, I turned into the
Strand. Again, at the Savoy, the same piles of stained
sandbags and a lone taxi made it seem forgotten.

But as I walked fast along the Strand, all devil-may-
care, I caught again the illusion of bravery, that surge
of audacity, of an act well-done in some private intrigue
of gallantry called "the war," was all safe, and for the
last time, except in echoes I would never believe again,
I stepped along with the deceptive simplicity of all romantics toward their duty in such dramatic form, a precious, innocent American Anglophile snob.

The WAAF clerk on duty at Kingsway recruiting station didn't look up when she said, "Name?" She motioned to a door. Just as she did, a military van drew up
outside. Two women Military Police, with a girl in civilian clothes slung between them, poured out of the
back of the van. The girl's legs were bare, filthy gray,
splashed with dried dirt like the dirty face of a child
finished crying. She had on heavy, solid, black Air-
Force issue shoes. I resolved that if I ran away I would
not wear issue shoes. The clerk saw me watching them

and ordered me through the door with a twinge of impatience. I realized then that there were several girls quietly queued behind me.

I can still recall, as hearing it again, the click of that washed, bare door closing. I was committed to, caught in among, a shy, tangle of very young-faced, very small girls standing against the walls, cowed by the waiting and the silence, shrinking a little from each other, just as I was shrinking away, isolated from them. Some of them were as dirty as the girl I had seen between the MP's. There, with the women in uniform at the recruiting station, we were a flotsam of intruders swept together by an order from a sergeant who walked in with that busy, slightly impatient, woman-on-the-job walk I was to know so well.

Manipulated by the sergeant, we stood in tattered, uneasy rows, twenty or so of us. An RAF officer came in. Through the embarrassment I could hear him, vaguely, explaining the oath of allegiance. Somewhere, out of a hundred and fifty years of revolution, a stop came to my American mind. I could join their forces, fight with them, try to do my duty, but I could not, would not, say the oath of allegiance to the King of England. It seemed important to cling to this in that minute, as the impersonal mutter of voices grew around me.

There must have been a bus to take us through London. That is gone from my memory. I stand again, as I stood then, in that snaggled row of women on a long blank platform of Paddington station, under the vast skeleton of its once-glass vault, now either bare to the sky or patched with black.

We were ushered onto the train. With the feeling of safety a railway journey always engenders in the British, a feeling of being able to escape commitment at the end, the girls in the carriage began to talk, or rather, to explain themselves to each other. They had something of the air of the woman traveling by public coach in a Dickens story who keeps explaining that her "postillion" will surely come to meet her, and their whole initial pride seemed to be in the fact that they wanted it to be understood that they were "volunteers"—this meaning, as I found out later, that they had joined up before the date of their call-up, so all of them in the carriage except the girl beside me must have been seventeen years old, and all except her were from the East End of London. Seeking to stand apart, she explained to me, or to whoever would listen, that she was from the suburbs—I have forgotten which one—and that she looked after her "mum," who was far from well, and that she was ever so worried about her, leaving her alone like that. It was the first glimpse of the stratification, almost Chinese in its complication and formality, which covered everything from a hairdo to a state of health to sugar in tea and by which each Englishman holds himself apart, himself his castle, from his fellows.

Unlike the East Enders, who wore their hair in high, hard unkempt wartime pompadours, her hair was marcelled in tight ridges close to her head, self-consciously "genteel." She kept touching it, pleased, and explained that she had been to the hairdresser's that morning and had had a "perm." In contrast to her tight, thin little body, holding itself up to its place by not even taking a deep breath, the other girls in the carriage, six of them, sprawled, easy in their East End solidarity, growing more and more pleased at the train ride.

I had no idea where we were going, north, south, east or west. No one had told me. I was afraid to open my American mouth and ask, partly since I suspected they would not understand me. Except for the girl with the "perm," whose voice was as careful as her body and who still spoke with a strong tinge of what I thought of as cockney, I could understand very little—a word here and there, as of a language not well known and spoken too fast—of what the East Enders were saying.

They sounded like six small Eliza Doolittles, sitting in rows, not giving a goddamn if they never learned to speak like "ladies"—far too proud to care. What I heard was something like "Coo wa a sayo—a flippin tunup." This, with a comfortable smile, was followed by an answer, "We aynt inem fer the lolly, sa bleedin seyo. Weyo we're bleedin forut naow," with a look of complacent agreement all round.

It was only when I caught the word "Reading" and saw the girl by the window opposite lean forward to see us come toward the town that I realized we were going west. The brackish, red-brick rows of houses began to slide by the windows as we slowed down. Here was something to understand: Reading—a literary pilgrimage. I leaned forward, too, studied the dull-looking town and spoke, hardly realizing it.

"Where's the jail?"

There was a dead silence. I watched the legs of the girl opposite, with the same gray surface of no sun and no scrubbing as all the others, feeling that I had shouted.

She said, "There," proudly and pointed to, I think, a slightly higher red roof jutting above the rest.

"Know someone there?" That incredible cockney came across to me, interested.

"No. Only about someone."

"Me bruver's in there," she said and leaned back, comfortable against the seat.

The train pulled out of Reading station.

"Wot was he 'ad up for, the fellow you know about?" she asked. I could almost see her toes wiggling with pleasure at someone to talk about to bridge the gap of strangeness.

But I'm afraid Oscar Wilde had to let us down.

"I don't know," I lied.

It was the deep early twilight of a rain-sodden evening when we got to the depot. I saw, in sunken, damp meadows under the heavy sky, a huddle of sterile-looking buildings, an imposed, square wartime design. We, in our civilian clothes, outsiders, without identity in such a new world, drew closer together as we shuffled along to a huge Nissen hut; other small groups of women were shuffling with us, silent with nervousness at the unknown, so when we got inside the hut, there must have been three hundred of us, jostled together, lost.

The light inside was naked, stripped. So was a woman's voice, bawling from the end of the hut for us to take off our clothes and line up. That impersonal command, taking away even the identity of clothes, was too shocking to leave time for humiliation. Stripped down, puny under the light, I looked around me and tears gathered behind my eyelids. I had never known before how food and habit developed a human body, how rare physical beauty was. All these very young products of the dole, then the war, of white bread, "marg" and strong tea, of a hard, city life already had the shrunken upper body, the heavy-set thighs, white and doughy, of mature women. No adolescent bodies rose lightly in that room—even the taken-for-granted litheness of the young girl was a luxury there. My own body, four years older, hard from sport and protein and sun, was as different from their hardness of survival as if I had been of a different species.

We lined up for an FFI—a Free From Infection. Each copying the one before, we lifted our arms to an unspoken order as we neared the medical orderlies. My head was jerked forward, my hair parted, pulled, my shaven underarms, my pubic hair inspected closely and completely, yet without any sense of human contact. I was ordered to get dressed.

Half of the women had been isolated into a group. I heard a sob from the other queue. It was the girl from the train with her new "perm," calling out to anyone who would notice, "I must 'ave leaned me 'ead back on the train. Those carriages are filthy."

When I was dressed and waiting, I asked a WAAF what was the matter with the others, who had been quickly herded into a farther room, out of sight. She laughed. "Most of them have nits—a few crabs," she told me. "They'll get a proper 'air cut and wash—good scrub down." I could see the new careful "perm" under the impatient medical scissors, the towering 1942 cockney headdresses piled on the bare floor.

"Half of them?" I said.

"This is a bloody clean lot compared to some." She forgot me and walked on down the bench, hurrying women back into their clothes.

Like lines of ants, a few joining a few more, combining gradually into a mainstream of movement, we grew into a mass, moving in the night mud, which sucked against our shoes, into long, long queues. Issue bedding, heavy, harsh brown blankets that smelled of dry hay, knives, forks, spoons, cups were heaped into our arms, while a WAAF stumped up and down the queue, yelling, "Any ST's? Any ST's?" and waving above her head a sanitary napkin from the bundle she carried. As she walked, stopping from time to time before some girl stumbling from need out of the privacy of a lifetime, her answer whispered in her shyness, the WAAF performed for us like one of those quick-talking "buskers" who entertain theater queues in London. I heard, for the first time, a new language even more unintelligible than that of the cockneys. It was the language of the Royal Air Force. The WAAF informed us at the top of her lungs that she was "browned" off, "brassed" off, that she'd " 'ad it"—that it had rained for a "fucking" week. This word, which I first heard used so casually by her, was the adjective of simplicity—the meaningless habitual definer. In real anger or passion it was hardly used, so that it had completely lost meaning. It was simply there, sprinkled in the conversation, as mild an expletive as spit.

The corners of the huge barnlike cookhouse disappeared beyond the dim, tin-shaded lights which made the ceiling recede into darkness, cavernlike. The mud from our shoes stayed wet on the concrete floor, and the wooden tables had a cold sweat to the touch. Two late for "tea," we ate the Air Force "supper"—sweet cocoa, slabs of bread and "marg." The drawn blackout curtains sagged, aged, greeny black, neglected and unnoticed after three years. Still clinging to a fast receding privilege of a private life, tired, cold, overshunted, we sagged at the tables, hardly looking at each other, quiet.

I glanced up once to see that at the end of the board, on the other side, a girl sat, looking as if she were spot-lit by her own color. She was yellow, a sort of inhu-man, chemical shade of yellow which had dyed her skin and her hair, which had fallen over her forehead from the rain and had made her look like a reconstruction of early man. Even her eyeballs, as she too stole a glance around her at the others, were yellow. As she moved, her broad shoulders and thick arms swelled against a dark, threadbare coat which could not have kept out the cold, much less the rain. I was repulsed by her looks and was afraid—and sorry, in a minute of shame, that my old camel's hair, chosen so carefully, must have seemed a point of luxury as glaring in the dimness as that strange yellow skin.

Trying to go to sleep the first night on three hard, square, straw-stuffed "biscuits" that made a mattress on the iron cot, one of the thirty set in two rows down the sides of the Nissen hut, I seemed to hear sounds until nearly morning—a hard, deep cough went on and on, somebody crying, quietly at first, then releasing the sobs of a child as whoever it was drifted nearer to sleep. The cold was the new, wet-fingered cold of England, which nothing could stop; it seemed to soak through the walls, up from the damp concrete floor, untouched by the small round iron stoves at either end of the hut in which wartime coke burned sullenly, giving neither light nor heat, only a sulfury smell. Not even the heavy, weighted blankets, my pajamas and my skin stopped the cold. It permeated to my bones and made me shake as if I had a fever. I wanted to cry like the unknown girl in the darkness, but knew it was no use. The warmth of Madame Prunier's seemed a lifetime instead of an afternoon away.

Before dawn, the Tannoy growled as if it were clear-ing its metal throat and a clipped, cool English voice roared through the hut.

"Ladies and gentlemen, it is 0600 hours."

For three days we seemed to be on a long march, ragged, tentative, jostling at first, gradually taking some kind of shape and ease, a melding, as we got used to walking together, being "oriented," tested and clothed in new stiff Air-Force-blue uniforms.

On the first day, while we were photographed like photographs in a jail, for our identity cards, we were given all-important serial numbers, at first on a clipboard pushed against our chins for the picture, then gradually tattooed on our brains. Old telephone numbers are gone, and addresses where I centered my life, but my serial number—2146391—and my rank—Aircraft Woman 2nd Class—are a part of identity, a scar that I will never lose. That identity, seeping through any former role, took over as the uniform began to set to my body, and the commands, the irresponsibility of being told every hour of the day what to do, became habit. Individual thought, another luxury, had to be buffed off. But that would be gradual, dangerous and unnoticed.

Over the crowd, waiting for the photographer, I saw the yellow girl again, a face standing out from the crowd by its color, dumb with patience.

The officer's war that I remembered receded so far from daily experience that when it was noticed at all, it seemed to intrude, blindly, interrupting the day. In the expedient blindness, the judicious lie so inculcated as a weapon of war in which the stupid and the vicious could hide as at no other time, the good officer stood out—direct as light.

On the day we were issued uniforms, we were marched past a high barbed-wire enclosure. Beyond it, WAAF walked two by two around and around an exercise yard cemented hard by feet. I saw none of them look up, even curiously, to make contact as we went past, not even when the corporal yelled, "Look out there. If you don't look lively, that's what will happen to you. You'll find yourself on the other side of that fence in detention." The girls inside walked on, in another world, without contact, their uniforms the dull, lighter gray cast of blue that was the color of the uniform when it was old and worn down.

I could not forget them. On leave, months later, I sat in evening clothes at a table at a Mayfair party in one of those deceptive intervals we like to remember as "the war," feeling comfortable in the softness of the voices and of civilian clothes, the telltale mark of the WAAF collar button, a constant pink spot on my throat, hidden by a necklace. I tried to tell the man beside me about it—about the women behind the wire. The woman opposite me interrupted in that voice of command I knew so well.

She said, "There are no WAAF detention barracks."

At first I didn't recognize the "policy" in her statement and answered, "But this is what I saw."

"There are no WAAF detention barracks," she said again and turned her head, the argument over. I saw then, above the low-cut evening dress, the pink mark of a WAAF collar button on her throat. She was a squadron officer at the Air Ministry. They probably called that dead, barbed-wire enclosure a kinder, more expedient, official name.

We were in uniform: a WAAF cap with a black, shining peak, a light-blue cotton shirt with a separate glossy hard collar, a black tie, a belted Air-Force-blue tunic, an Air-Force-blue skirt at the regulation ten inches from the ground, thick cotton Air-Force-blue stockings, heavy black shoes and, under it all, issue Air-Force-blue rayon bloomers to our knees, a white cotton undershirt, a "corset cover—WAAF for the use of," to quote King's Regulations on the issue brassiere. Over it all, we wore the heavy, well-designed Air-Force-blue greatcoat.

We were no longer undefined flotsam at the depot. Late into the night we polished the dull, new buttons and the brass insignia on our caps, so that they would begin to get the sheen of wear and time so envied in the older brass of the corporal. Spit and polish, every old wives' tale, or old soldiers', for polishing brass was used. What began to work was the incessant movement of rags over the insignia on our buttons, the hypnotic movement of our knuckles back and forth over the cleaning racks, the pleating of our caps so they would not stand up like chef's caps but lie flat, the bending and kneading of the thick, hard shoes, in which I felt, those first few days, as if I were being asked to walk across England with my feet in stone.

Then, in the language of the Air Force—whose motto, *"Per Ardua ad Astra,"* reached from the sky and the swooping Spitfires to the arduousness of my sore feet—we were formed into "flights" to be posted to initial training units. This time, dragging still-white canvas kitbags and in our new WAAF greatcoats, we formed a unit on the platform and in the train.

I swayed along the platform, weighted down by the clothes and the loaded kitbag. Whatever attempts I made to become part ot it all were still only conscious. My stomach, which had quietly refused the fat-soaked food that smelled of garbage, the glutinous masses of porridge, the thick, stewed tea, had gone into a revolt of its own and allowed me to hold down no food for nearly a week. And sleep itself is our safe state of anarchy. My body, when it touched sleep, would thrash against the hard blankets and the "biscuits," throwing the center one half out toward the floor, casting off the blankets wrapped around them to anchor them and letting in the cold, which would keep me just under wakefulness for the rest of the night, just under the decision to get up and touch the icy floor with my feet and remake my bed. So, without much food or sleep for a week, I felt light-headed and floating in fatigue; I tried and failed to lift the kitbag to throw it into the carriage.

Someone grabbed my kitbag and I grabbed back, instinctively, without looking.

" 'Ere, come on," the comfortable, rough voice beside me had the impatience of a busy mother. The kitbag was wrested from me and tossed onto the train. It was the yellow-skinned girl. She jumped up after it, and I followed.

Divisions were made, quickly—at first, divisions of survival, of coming together for safety. I had hardly spoken a word to anyone during the week, and no one had to me. I found no friend to fall in beside and walk along with to the cookhouse, no one to complain with. I thought it was me; I had not yet learned that the xeno-phobia of the English is deep—not so much a phobia as an instinctive withdrawal before the stranger, usually broken down in wartime. But in these circumstances of too much strangeness, it was harsh and strong with self-protection. Among the others, especially after the flight had been formed, it was easy to move along into pro-tective groups—a street, a district, gestures, voices, all were like hooks to hang together with. The East Enders were the majority, and they formed a solid phalanx. I envied their security, a kind of enjoyment I could hear from them across the hut, at the cookhouse tables, in the ablutions. But I had no hooks out that they could trust. I was all stranger, and quite literally, in language, they could not understand me, nor I them.

So when the drift within the flight began, I had thought I was not drifting with it, but I was, as much as the others. The tendrils, the communications of the "odd man out," by the time we got into the carriage, had formed a protective group of its own and had swept me along with it. Its first sign was the rather timid and formal exposure of first names—a sign of privacy in a whole life where one was known only by one's last name—usually yelled out.

Viv, from Liverpool, was "named for me mum. We're from Liverpool. We're Protestants." She told us this with the shy definition the English have within their labyrinthine class system, which stated social gulfs and prides of self I could not yet read. She had been a worker in a munitions factory until she was let go be-cause the fumes had begun to poison her. The poison, which had dyed her skin yellow, had already, in a week, begun to fade out of her eyes. Her arms, which had been able to throw my kitbag onto the train so lightly, were, from heavy work in the factory, as developed as a man's. What had been a frightening quality in her hard, ugly face, grew into a sort of kindly, doggy, ugliness as she became familiar in the uniform and as the yellow faded. She moved like a steamroller, carrying within her the timidity of a not-quite-domesticated animal.

At first I thought that the rarity of the two sitting beside Viv was because of their beauty, certainly a rarity among women en masse. The first, Tina, had that fine profile of face and body that Americans identify with English aristocrats and which is so seldom seen. Already her ill-cut WAAF uniform fitted her like hunting clothes. I had noticed her first because she was as tall as I was, so that our eyes met, without recognition, over the heads of the others as we were crowded in and out of the buildings of the depot. Now she flung down her cap with one arrogant gesture of her long hand and tossed her head, loosening her short, lank, shining blond hair. That was the first level of impression of her—at once the second level intruded and both destroyed and explained it. Her eyes were dead, bitter and flat, as if when she was a child she had exposed her elegant face to the pity of people who had no pity and would never do it again. Her mouth was not cruel—that was too positive—but closed, finely formed and bitter. When she told us her name, she said, "Clementina Beaumont Scruggs-hyphen-Smith," as if it were a joke.

The second said, "I'm Penny," as if that were a joke too, but another kind. She was a vicar's daughter from Devonshire with the only true-lavender eyes I have ever seen, a perfect pink-and-white soft skin, a small, pretty pink mouth like a Romney, delicate hands and feet, a halo of blond curls. In uniform, she was already reasserting herself as a woman, wearing the androgynous clothing as a joke. She wore her cap as if it were her lover's. Every physical thing about her was a nose-thumb at the Air-Force-blue conformity. Her eyes worked even on the color, making it charming. She had been in the land army. Out of that rose-petal mouth, from the time she sat down in the carriage until we were posted to different stations after initial training, there came, quite joyfully and with perfect friendliness, a stream of language so foul it was a constant education. It came from rebellion against some vicarage I would never see, from the stable and the pig pen, like the creature in the fairy tale who poured out frogs when she spoke. She had the cot beside me for six weeks. Every morning, when the Tannoy ceased to really wake me, I would hear from dreams to reality a sort of educating blasphemous, obscene, paean into wakefulness and would open my eyes to see that Penny's small feet, with their pink-shell toenails, had hit the damp, freezing concrete floor.

We were assigned to our hut. We had already learned to race for position, near the ablutions, near the stove, in a protective corner which was to take on an identity, jealousy guarded, of home for a while. Viv raced ahead of us, flung her kitbag on one bed, her cap on another, her greatcoat on a third and her own bottom on a fourth. She stared with such fierce protectiveness that no one dared to take the fifth cot. Gradually the rest of the hut filled with clankings and groans, voices were raised as they had never been at the depot as we stowed our kits and began to retrieve the few precious personal belongings we could have with us—a few photographs, a "torch," makeup (rare, guarded fiendishly and almost impossible to replace), knitted scarves and gloves of Air-Force-blue wool some had brought with them.

Then, through all the noise, grumbling and whickering as she pulled her kitbag along the floor, came the fifth of us, ignoring Viv's stare as she dropped her gear in a pile, flung the biscuits flat on the cot, collapsed on them and whimpered, "Dear heavenly holy merciful *God*." At her shoulders were already carefully sewn flashes reading "Eire." This was Paddy, carrying, turtlelike, so there could be no mistaking her, the impossible Irish music-hall name of Siobin O'Sullivan. When she had recovered from moving, she began (toward us, the cockneys on the other side of her ignoring her as if she didn't exist), in a comfortable bourgeois educated Dublin voice that poured over us like soft water, a sorrowful story of volunteering for the English Forces be-

cause she had had a bloody fight with her husband, and
that it was already the worst bloody mistake of her
bloody life and that she ached and suffered in bones she
hadn't known existed before in a bloody beautiful home
she'd never survive to see again. By the time she paused
for breath, which she seemed to have seldom to do, all
of us but Viv were helpless with laughter. Paddy was
one of those natural comics who transmute any disaster
to comedy simply by putting it through their brains
and mouths—always sadly, always with a complaint, already condemned not to be taken seriously. It was a
good thing for true perspective on disaster that Paddy
was not the first survivor ashore from the sinking of the
Titanic.

RAF Hereford, the initial training unit, lay imposed
on Herefordshire meadows of that incredibly bright
green even in the late fall, of west-country grazing land,
deep with mud, and dank. In the far distance, when the
mist rose at midday, we could see the Malvern Hills. I
wondered if it were accident or design to set us so low
in the stripping down of the depot that when we had
formed companies and had begun to learn drill our
pride resurged, no longer so personal, but a growing
corps pride. Marching with the others, the loss of self
and the gain of communal pleasure came without realization. Arms flung out straight, in a proud, precise
group stride, we marched down the roads between the
low hutments to the parade ground, while the men attached to the station stopped along the side and whis-
tled "Bollucks, and the same to you," which I found out
much later was called "Colonel Bogey," or an equally
familiar British march with the whispered other ranks
words, "Ain't it a pity she's only one titty to feed the
baby with."

Tina and I, being the tallest, led the company; she
kept up, so low I could hardly hear it, a running sore of
talk, simple and terrible, a sort of unredeemed comment on her life. Her mother had died when she was
small and she had been brought up in poverty and with
perverted pride by a father who had been wounded in

the First World War, one of those ex-officers who can never find a place in peacetime and who fester with bitterness toward their country and their fate. His only pride had been in being a member of Mosley's Fascist party. He sounded typical of those dangerous, pretentious members, fallen there by circumstance, of the paranoid cliff-hangers just above the morass of Britain's lower middle classes, clinging to their hatreds, their self-appointed hyphens and, always, to some vague and tenuous connection with a bishop, a general or a minor peer. Ironically, all the pretension of her father had been parodied in Tina's looks and in the way, even though she hated any duty toward what she called "they" (those who "had all the advantages"), she stepped out on parade with a physical pride that matched her looks, looking as though she were marching to burn the Reichstag.

Just behind us marched Viv, doggedly listening, watching both of us as if we were some sort of exotic animals she could not try to understand, only watch and, as it happened later, watch over. Sometimes, when we fell onto our cots at the end of the day, Tina complaining, Penny swearing delicately, like the sound of little bells, Paddy groaning and reaching for the inevitable "fag," Viv would join in the talk with stories dredged up to match what we were saying.

Like Eliza Doolittle, Viv had once, she told us with pride, ridden in a taxi. We prepared to make those kindly noises people make to interrupting children who want to join in but have not quite caught the drift of the conversation, when she went on, proudly, that her husband had beaten her up, stolen her radio and gone off to take ship. The police drove her in a taxi "all the way to the docks" to arrest him. "I got back me wireless, too," she finished, taking all these facts of life for granted. Viv was proud of being married, even though she hadn't seen her husband for two years and didn't know whether he was alive or dead. I think she took my look of shock at her story as the pleased surprise she expected for having ridden in a taxi, for she ended her story with, "I did then. All the way to the docks."

After the story, we had no more to say. I fell to that incessant polishing of shoes and buttons' that in the Forces acts like a kind of Yoga hypnosis, replacing thought or despair or future. Paddy turned away from Viv, embarrassed, and began the long feminine ritual she went through every night, putting her short wiry hair in a thousand little pins, covering it with an old-fashioned pink boudoir cap, covering her face with a white herbal cream, dressing herself in a quilted robe and handknitted bed socks with wool roses. There was something so incongruous and sad about her going to bed that even Paddy didn't seem comic, only typical of those clinging to tender and private habits in the midst of all that impersonal exposure.

I still had the illusion, common to artists at moments of registering concentration and to the isolated in cities, that I was observing all that was going on around me without being noticed, except by my own few comrades in despair, complaint and constant discomfort. They had made a whole new world for me. Walking along in the pitch dark two hours before daylight, with the double-daylight saving time of the short days so far north, I was no longer alone. I could hear Paddy fall in beside me, murmuring, instead of "It's fucking cold" like most of the others, "Aye, the bloody mist is rising and falling over the hills and valleys of this bloody benighted country."

In the cookhouse the smell of sleep, sweat and damp wool mingled with the sick-animal smell of the food, the sweet medicinal smell of the long-boiled tea. By the third morning I could see several of the cockney girls look up when we came in, disinterested. I took no notice of being singled out.

Perhaps we were noticed first because we were enough different to be remembered from the others. Perhaps it was because the intelligence tests taken at the depot had frightened most of the others into being more inarticulate than what I would find out later was their high degree of natural quickness, their surviving intelligence. Tina, Penny and I, who had seen such tests before, made a better showing. That morning we were singled out for interviews for Officer's Training School. To the rest, as we left the orientation lecture, we were only noticed for the difference, criminal if left unexplained, of being set apart.

At any rate, from that minute my isolation was gone, replaced by an active withdrawal, a turning away, as if strangeness were a communicable disease. Tina, detesting them and herself, and Penny, dancing with her obscene twittering through it all, already used to dealing with a life like the WAAF in the land army, could give as good as they got, could flick back remarks in the ablutions, fighting for the cold water in a common language. Paddy had the grace of making them laugh, lugubrious in her self-protection. To me, the talk was still as alien as Urdu. I was struck dumb by it and replaced talk with the retreat of the liberal snob into "they're not knowing any better" and with the decision that I would have to go 75 per cent of the way toward them because of "my advantages." I did this with a puppy-dog smile whenever one or two of them jostled into me, flinging me out of the way of the water tap or of what I was learning to call the "lou."

I had noticed the other habits of privacy, but, of course, I had not noticed my own. The reek of unwashed bodies with their underwear kept on for a week was sickening. They in turn saw me night after night strip down to what was to them the obscenity of complete nakedness before I put on my harsh, striped WAAF pajamas. I took to going, before the call "Ladies and gentlemen, it is 0600 hours," out into the rain, which never seemed absent in the early morning, to the showers, where there was hot water only from six to six-thirty, and taking a hot shower. In the cookhouse I refused the soggy porridge with an upturning of my nose I could not control. I received no letters and, because of having no money, never went with the rest to drink the watery beer in the NAAFI, which was the recreation center of the RAF station, but sat in the evening in the station library reading the thumbed, torn wartime paperbacks.

I volunteered, having had no training to call out of my past but the Girl Scouts and a camp in Virginia where jollity and helpfulness, admired and envied in older "honor girls," had been inculcated in me like a virus and a wholly American education that the early bird got the worm. I had yet to learn the first rule, command, dogma of being an other rank in the Forces, or, I'm sure, of being in any authoritarian or conformist state: Never volunteer, never stand out. I learned it quickly. Even the sergeant who asked for "a volunteer" grinned when I stood up.

"Take the ST's out of the ablutions and burn them," she ordered loudly. There was a wave of snickering from the others. I could feel my face burning. The early bird had gotten not the worm, but half a ton of used sanitary napkins. I turned to leave the lecture room. "No, not now," the sergeant ordered, "in your off time." I found out later that this was usually one of the WAAF "jankers"—the RAF term for punishment fatigues.

When I went into the first ablution, the sanitary-towel bin was empty. All down the lines of ablutions behind the huts I could find nothing but empty bins. Then I looked up onto the hill in the distance. A lone figure stood in front of a bonfire, the air above it dancing with invisible flames. I ran up. It was Viv. She watched me climb the hill and shut me up with a short "Will you ever keep your gob stopped? This is never for the likes of you—can't even eat the food . . ." She received my heartfelt thanks with such fierceness that I trudged off down the hill again, leaving her standing in the mist.

Finally we were paid—ten shillings—and given time off. The bus going into Hereford was overflowing with WAAF, singing loudly, as military as only women could be, self-conscious in their new role, freed for the first afternoon since joining up. They, in their new military role in public, called out the Forces' insult to civilians out of the bus windows, "Ah, you dirty civic, get some in!," the "some" being time in the service, of which they had had about three weeks. I went alone. It was my first chance to see an English town, and I wanted to wander through it instead of going with the others to the "flicks."

It was already afternoon. In half an hour I had broken my newly inculcated military stride and was wandering around the small and delicate tenth-century Hereford cathedral, gawking at the mixture of nineteenth-century Reconstruction and Early English, not able to tell them apart. As I walked along the high street of Hereford later I saw a shop with military dress; in the window were piles of flashes: Eire, Canada, NZ, Australia and two, amazingly, reading "USA." I bought them with too much of my ten bob, some writing paper and a bag of "sweets." It was already late afternoon, and I wandered into a pub to watch the RAF men, or boys rather, from the station play darts. I sat quietly, drinking a small, warm beer. Several of them came and sat down at the table, polite, disinterested, more involved in the dart game. The swinging doors of the saloon bar opened, and two WAAF I recognized from the hut looked in. One of them was a pinched-faced girl with one of those pointed English noses which looks like it has a questing life of its own. She was almost emaciated. I had wondered how she stood the constant drill without fainting. I smiled and half waved. They let the doors swing together again. I thought they hadn't seen me.

It was time to go back to the station, and I still had two shillings six pence for the next week. The hut was empty. I got out my "housewife" and sewed my USA flashes on my uniform shoulders, wandered away to late tea and on to the library to write letters, having at last time enough to think through what had happened and sift it down to a letter setting a lying tone of amusement to a world that could not have the least idea of what it was like there in the empty Nissen hut, with the black-out curtains already pulled and my Air-Force-blue sleeve moving over the onionskin air-mail form. The letters were finished. I was relaxed and at peace from the afternoon's letting-go. It was nine o'clock. The train had started again. I picked my way alone through the wetness, protecting the letters and my new-bought sweets under my groundsheet, avoiding the deep puddles that days of rain had made soft with hidden mud. Through the blackout I counted the vague outlines of the huts until I came to my own. When I started up the six steps to the door, counting them carefully in the dark to keep from stumbling, I saw that it was open. The flick of the blackout curtain let out a pencil of light that lit my face and disappeared again. It was dead quiet.

I pushed open the curtain. Something fell against me like a dead weight, too quickly to frighten me or, fortunately, for me to tense my muscles. I felt myself grabbed by my arms and legs and flung out in an arc into the empty air like a sack of grain. I landed on my back in a large puddle in the soft mud. My letters flew out of sight; my sweets were gone. There was a roar of noise. In the door above me stood a mass of WAAF, yelling. One, the leader, the little pinched-faced girl, kept calling over the others, "That'll teach the fuckin' toffy-nose."

Something broke, and it wasn't a bone. It was the massed fury against the ignominy of all the brave promises, all the decision, ending up flat on my back in the rain with my cap rolled away in the dark, my few treasures lost and a bunch of drunken foreign conscripts yelling at me. Out of me rumbled a fury all the way from Morgan's raiders and a language I didn't know I knew. I just lay there on the ground and swore until there was a dead silence. Then, knocking the others into each other, down the steps came Viv and Tina, clearing them out.

"If it gets me twenty-eight days CC I'll murder you," Viv was yelling. They picked me up. The letters had sunk in the mud; the sweets were gone. Fury was melting toward tears.

"Don't let the buggers see you cry," Tina said and jerked at my arm.

We walked into the barracks. The usually clean, dead-looking hut was a bacchanal. Drunken girls danced on the cots, for once unafraid of Viv or the kind little round corporal who had appeared in her door and was trying to make herself heard.

The pinched-faced girl was jumping up and down on her cot. When she saw me she screamed, "You think we're a dirty lot, with your baths and your bare body. Oo wants to look at it? A ten-bob tart's wot you are. We seen you getting trade in the pub! She's a ten-bob tart from up west."

I supposed she'd set my price at ten bob because that was the largest sum we could think of on our first pay day, my job as prostitution because, to their minds, there could be no other reason for my mystery and my home as "up west," the West End of London, because that was as far away, as glamorous, as "toffy-nosed," as a seventeen-year-old East Ender could imagine. I didn't know then that ten bob was the top going price in 1942.

Viv pulled me into the corporal's room and slammed the door against the noise. I stood pouring mud onto the corporal's floor while they helped my groundsheet over my streaming mud-soaked hair. My forehead had been cut—how I don't know. Mud, tears and blood splattered my face. I kept saying, "What have I done? I don't know what I've done," as if in that few minutes they could answer the questions of all strangers, all who drew attack in the world, from wounded chickens to Jews.

Tina took off my greatcoat and the corporal saw the USA flashes on my shoulders. "Well, I'll be buggered," was all she said.

Later, we marched through the barracks to the ablutions. The noise was over, the long room calm, dark except for the red glow from the stoves, where we had already learned to make the coke glow with liberal doses of Brasso. We went into the ablutions, with the one dim blackout bulb burning, to wash my hair in the cold water and clean my face.

In bed, waiting to sleep, the women in the room were awake but dead quiet. I knew they were listening. So did Viv and Penny, who had missed the fight, to her own fury. From her bed I heard a last mutter, "Bugger the lot of them."

I said, "Ten bob, for God's sake!"

Out of the darkness on the other side came Viv's voice, admiring and sad, "That's a lot, isn't it? I was a waitress in a house once. But they didn't get that. I couldn't be nothing but a waitress. Not good-looking enough. But I got smashing tips."

Chapter 3

News traveled fast from 0600 hours through breakfast. The next mid-morning I marched toward the parade ground for square bashing at the front corner of the flight. Tina was beside me, and a third girl, her clenched hand thrusting with a cutting movement at the air as she marched, was driving her fist into the corner of my vision as, eyes front, we stepped out down the gray road. I had a bruise on my right cheekbone which looked like dirt I hadn't managed to clean away. I was wracked by a deep cough from the cold-water shampoo of the night before, so as I marched I concentrated on making my bladder behave, jarred by the cough, as we passed through a corridor of the men of the camp, now whistling *Yankee Doodle*.

I, bladder, bruise and all, was cold, happy and triumphant. No one that morning had pushed me out of the way of the cold tap. One girl, brass blond, painting a new coat of lipstick over yesterday's lips, had even, out of the corner of her mouth, said, "Wotcher?" and grinned as I stood beside her, brushing my teeth, still in my WAAF underwear of the day before, aware of my own warm smell. At breakfast someone moved and made room for me to step over the bench and sit near the middle of one of the dank trestle tables.

Able to act by looking, instead of avoiding being looked at, at last, I noticed that the girls around me had begun to fill out and glow. Their skin was losing its thickness. They looked seventeen. In what seemed to me a life without joy which was imposed on most of them without their choice, they were beginning to thrive. The days that had stripped me of weight, well-being and habit so soon were acting on them in the opposite way. Air, exercise, regular meals and the very act for some of them of sleeping above ground for the first time in years were making the blood run better through their bodies.

I saw all this without conversion, only with horror that such a life, such indifferent regimentation, such ciphering, was better than they had known before. It presented a terrible social excuse. I saw, as a twinge at the corner of my mind, how fascism feeds the unconscious body and how the luxury of freedom without responsibility can produce a twisted body somewhere as a dark mirror for every healthy, privileged one.

Through the corridor of *Yankee Doodle* we came to the parade ground. The morning air in the new after-breakfast dawn was tinged white from our breath over the flat space of the square; through it in the distance the yell of a sergeant seemed to float over the stamp of feet as we dressed ranks, wheeled, counted, slapped shoes, hollow sounding on the concrete, snapped turns, "By the *right*, qui-ick *mach*." I thought of Kipling, of all the roles, the acquiescence to orders yelled in the same cockney voice, all the way from Danny Deever to ACW Settle. It was very romantic that morning. The slaps grew louder on the pavement, the arms thrust higher, square bashing went on faster, lighter, euphoric, impersonal, all movement and sound, no person, without body. A yell cut through the air, "Halt! Ri-ight turn. AT EASE." The word "ease" melted through my body; losing the stiffness in the inverted V of my legs thrust toward the concrete, I slowly, calmly turned toward the sky.

I woke up at the side of the parade ground, looking at the sun's shadow through the white haze, and fell in again to march to the orientation lecture. Tina grumbled. "Left you on the ground until the sergeant finished, they did"—her cockney creeping into her angry voice—"What do they think we are, fucking Guardsmen?"

I shut out her incessant voice, because I felt delicate and fine, and concentrated on marching with my new paper legs, relieved that in the giving up of consciousness my bladder hadn't given up too, but had remained Puritan, trained and dependable, even in a dead faint.

"I'm going to work my ticket," Tina said, finishing whatever she was saying as we filed into the lecture room. I heard that because I didn't yet know what it meant. Tina had already picked up more of the language.

"What?" I whispered.

"Not here, you silly clot, no officers," she said.

It was good to sit inside the Nissen hut for a few minutes, under the curved corrugated iron roof, watching it to keep from looking at anyone, with the sergeant yelling "Quiet" every time a giggle burbled up. The word was getting around that we were going to have a sex lecture, and every new girl it got to gave a short burp of a giggle. At every sound Viv, as stern that morning as an NCO, jerked around and scowled. She had taken the orientation lectures seriously since the one on God. It had been given by a tiny, handsome Scot, a Presbyterian padre who had begun by saying, "I'm no' here to talk about games, I'm here to talk about God." He had said it sternly and had proceeded to carry out his promise, with kindness and courage in the face of a Nissen hut full of agnostic girls, all larger than himself. Viv had fallen into a kind of admiring love with him and planned to go and talk to him about her problems when she could think up what they were. We talked at night, trying to help her decide. For three days she had taken the lectures seriously, thinking, from the padre, that all officers were there to help, as if his presence were somehow in all the officers' uniforms.

We were pulled to our feet by the yell " 'Tension!' Behind us I could hear the parody of a soldier's stride as the "Admin" officer marched alone down the aisle. She marched up the steps to the stage, her swagger stick thrust under her arm. Then she snapped a turn, slapped the swagger stick across her palm, creased her face into a silent smile and said, "At ease, girls," and stood to a rigid at-ease herself as she watched us slurp back into our seats.

She was spare and lean, birdlike on stalk legs; her breasts were thrust together under her meticulous tight tunic so that she presented a unilateral, slightly swollen front. Through the whole lecture she never moved her head, straight on her thin neck above her absolutely centered tie, her officer's cap straight on her pulled-back Eton crop. She looked as if the only sex she had experienced was a flipped towel in a locker room, but, oh, what jolly-brave fellow-girl would have had the nerve?

She began with a scare campaign in all its Lesbian horror which would have thrown anyone but the most passionate sensualist off sex forever, if anyone had listened. She clipped out information about disease—this was so far from the delightful subject we all had expected that I could hear the hum and fidget around me of minds wandering. She told about crabs, warned about toilet seats, skipped over prophylactics, urged antiseptics, pictured tertiary paralysis. The swagger stick kept on slapping, punishing her bad left hand with her good right hand.

"My girls"—she slapped—"are honorable [slap, slap], clean [slap, slap]." The room hummed with boredom.

"There are married women among my girls"—she slapped—"In the event of pregnancy [fire, catastrophe, act of God] you are released from active duty at the termination of three months." I looked around at Tina, who was smiling. I knew what "working one's ticket" meant.

"Many of my girls join up again after the event." The "Admin" officer said all this with the official insistence in her voice that demanded that all children be conceived after wedlock, in the "marital position," as a duty, in bed at night.

"Not bloody likely," Tina muttered.

Then the hatchet face hardened. It darkened, drew in, as if her whole face were at the mercy of her next words.

"There are foreign troops in the country," she stated, as if she had just discovered and was loath to announce that the small island was bulging with Allies. "They have more money . . ." I began to realize that she was talking about American soldiers. The room warmed toward interest.

"I can't *stop* you meeting them. But one thing I must warn you about. I absolutely forbid my girls being seen talking to American niggers."

I felt my face tense as if it had been slapped. I was stripped by that cold voice, opened, exposed, my barriers down to an inrush of terror and loss. I had run from those hard mouths all the way from America. What I had escaped from to war had followed me, the mouths grinning around "bunchajews," "bunchaniggers," to catch me, pinned there in the lecture room, that hard face—certain, secure and unjust—swimming before my eyes. I knew that there was no place, no country where I would not find it, that the brutality of mind we fight, we fight in the country of the mind. It is every place; it is not political, but is an act of darkness, sometimes in power, sometimes suppressed, always to be fought. Later I would have a middle-class English Community try to convert me by telling me that there was anti-Semitism in the Soviet Union, as if that made them "all right."

I thought that what I had done was a useless, ironic sacrifice, that I had kept my appointment in that cold, functional Nissen hut only by avoiding it at home. Almost everyone had begged of me a cheap reason to understand my action—a man, money—never knowing that however mistaken the carrying-out may be, there had been a flash, a sense of right, that can guide the minutes of one's life and make one turn. Stripped of that sense, I could only watch the woman's mouth, finishing with that assumption of ownership found in those of her class when they lack the perception to know that the core of dignity is the recognition of another's freedom.

"On the whole, I'm proud of my girls. You'll find them a jolly fine lot." Her mouth stretched into a last smile, and she snapped it into attention again. I kept paraphrasing a poem I'd heard: "The Fascist lady is so refined. She has no bosom and no behind."

We stood as she processed up the aisle, forgetting us. Then, as we marched out of the lecture room to form ranks in the road, I heard one WAAF say to another, "She's not fucking well going to tell *me* 'oo to see!" I had forgotten the anarchy of the unknown people, their saving dumb insolence, that effective impotence.

At the door the sergeant told me to report to sick bay that I had fainted on parade.

The girl with the "perm" who had sat beside me on the train was crouched at the end of the wooden waiting bench in the sick bay. Her uniform seemed not to touch her anyplace. She had shrunk inside it, the stiffness which had been her gentility crumbled. Her hair was cut in a short pudding-bowl shape around her thin skull. Her eyes were enormous and vacant. She didn't pretend to recognize me when I sat down beside her, but began, continuing as if she had never left the train and this was all a dream, the dreary recitation of her mum's being bad and how she was bad (ill) half the time herself and could hardly carry on. She conjured up a sad, thin, *folie à deux* of two paper women in oatmeal handknitted jumpers, protecting their dry lungs, wandering with a dim, slow trudge in a vague drugged haze of patent medicine and, when they could get them, comforting stronger tonics from some hard-worked GP.

After the induced mild madness of mum and the medicine cabinet, she was not withstanding the reality of the last three weeks. Both of us sat there with that in common, our hands shaking slightly in our laps.

A medical orderly put his head out of the medical officer's door and grinned when he saw her.

"Go on back, luv, 'e's not seeing you today. You've 'ad yours," he told her.

She got up as if she were in pain.

"It was a laxative," she forced the embarrassing words out of her dry mouth. "I need something for me 'ead."

"Get along, luv." He watched her leave, then said, "She's a bed wetter. Bet it's bloody cold. That lot don't last."

I was ordered into the medical officer's room. He told me to get a hold on myself and to stop washing in hot water until I got used to the weather, and he gave me a No. 9, which I, knowing already that it was a strong laxative, didn't take.

That night we talked late in the corner, whispering after lights-out in a parody of boarding-school life. Penny and I sneaked out to smoke a fag in the ablutions. We heard a scream from two ablutions away, the kind of scream that made us run toward it. Two or three girls were already fighting through the door as we got to it.

Inside the ablutions, the blackout light made huge shadows of the struts around the toilets. The shadows were arched along the concrete ceiling. Below the arches was the shadow of a large, long bundle, hanging by a cord, moving around and around slowly. I saw it only for a second. Large shadow hands reached up to cut the bundle down.

It was the girl with the "perm." She had hanged herself by the cord of her WAAF pajamas to one of the toilet struts. She was not dead. When we got to her, she began to moan. In a few minutes she was sitting up. She had no idea where she was. She had shut us out, shut out all the blue-gray and the fog, the concrete and the cold. She kept smiling, very sweetly, servile and sympathetic, at something in the empty air as the corporal who had cut her down guided her out of the ablutions into the dark toward the sick bay. We never saw her again.

That was one way out. Tina, quite coolly, set out to take the other way, but I could only see this in the memory of her voice muttering, "I'm going to work my ticket," for her actions were covered, even for herself, by a cocoon of wartime romance. I first noticed Tina's use of her WAAF pajamas, which, when she came back from her third afternoon in town, she took out of her canvas gas-mask case and threw on her cot. The corners of her pajama jacket were wrinkled from being tied in a tight knot under her breasts. It was the only way to make that striped flannel glamorous, and it would become the visible and outward sign that the WAAF with the wrinkled pajamas was sleeping with a man. Tina, for her own reasons and in her own way, had fallen in love.

She told about it with her face pink with pleasure and embarrassment. He was in training to be a bomber pilot. They had met at the flicks. No one recognized anything as unromantic and civilian as a pickup. They were in uniform, thrown together in the kinship of service by the war. As other couples do, confident for a while that the circumstances of the world will go their way, Tina and her pilot officer planned a future as they took the few hours off duty together in the cold rooms of wartime boarding houses or out-of-the-way pubs.

On the cots at night, with only the glow from the coke stove lighting her fine face, Tina would carry these dreams back to us—how if you worked it right you could make a good thing out of the war, how her fiancé's brother had gotten out of Belgium in 1940 fat with forty yards of Brussels lace wrapped around his body under his uniform. Such grand visions would make Tina lie back, her hands behind her blond head, staring up at the light of the stove on the hut ceiling, wishing and waiting for Paragraph Eleven.

Born to face life as it was, hard edged, without any experience of the soft contours of "how it ought to be," Viv took Tina's dreams as part of the "just lovely" aspect of reality. They had in common the conventions of a submerged world, and those conventions were as strong as any hard rules to protect the pretensions of the less realistic and more comfortable. It was as if the "rules" were the same, but they governed exigencies I didn't know existed and attitudes I had never been forced to take. By Viv they were simply accepted, by Tina they were manipulated, in that division found at every level between the exploitive and the simple hearted.

Then shyly, needing, as all people in romantic states do, approval, Tina asked me to meet her pilot officer.

He was sitting, watching the door, as we came into the pub at Windhallow-over-Water, one of those nine-house villages strung along a wide main road, neither lovely nor memorable, whose shedlike public house was suddenly made the focus of troops in the area. The pub retained its deserted ugliness with all the stubbornness of the old men who were its main customers in peace-time. Two of them sat on a wooden bench, leaning against the plaster wall below the worn dart board, ignoring us, staring beyond us out the open door toward the road, deserted of cars by the war.

Nina's pilot officer sprang up when he saw us and stood, crouched behind the trestle table, to be introduced. Tina did it with a touching new gentleness, her mouth small with politeness. We sat down.

No one said a word.

The old men and the old men's pub threatened to defeat us. I was doubly on edge because I knew that they were aware of having sacrificed the beginning of a rare afternoon in bed for the meeting. To save ourselves from the silence, Tina and I fell upon stories about Viv, Tina bringing out her whole trained-bear quality, dissecting it as we played lady to her pilot's gentleman, using Viv as the convenient peasant we had to suffer—I, ashamed guest, acquiescing and drinking the warm, watery beer. At the time, I saw them clearly, but only after years do I see myself clearly too, laughing with them at Viv, being a polite coward, while over our heads the Oxford training planes rumbled through the still air like the rolling of empty barrels.

The pilot officer relaxed, expanded and joined in the talk, speaking of the lower "clarses" with an exaggerated hard "r," imitating his own voice. He had managed to turn his uniform into a sort of costume for his vision of himself—cap crushed back, tunic rigorously casual, luxuriant moustache and, under the disguise, thin arms, hands nervously playing with his glass and suddenly throwing it to his hidden mouth; his draining it with his Adam's apple bobbing, then shouting "Drink up!" as if we were a whole pub full of pilots saving England instead of two WAAF and two old men in the pale, diffused light from the road playing across the ceiling and the bar. Each time he shouted, the old woman who ran the pub would come in from some cavern at the back, wiping her hands, and take our glasses without a word or a smile.

Within an hour, out of relief after the polite tension and glass after glass of weak beer, we managed to make ourselves slightly drunk. Tina and her young man were jovial, but they were jovial about the same bitter criticisms of the world I had heard her pour out for weeks. In what unknown disguises the known returns to us! Tina was showing me, with all the pride of escape from the past, a replica of her father, as if the source of her bitterness would have to be fed all through her life. I could see that young man, with all his jokes about the "lower clarses" and the "Yids"—if he survived the war at all—going from one slightly shady job to another, growing more rigid in his resentment, looking back on this war, perhaps even on this pale afternoon when they sat, happily feeding on each other and the hatred of "they," as the best years of his life.

"Working her ticket" was, I'm sure, completely submerged in Tina's mind. I could see the original reason for action pushed underground as the illusions of the action took over, necessity becoming the illusion of choice, manipulation recognized as "fate" and, at its best, the demand for life surging forth, flooding the barriers and later becoming submerged in a channel of conventional behavior.

I cannot tell what happened to Tina. Within two weeks I was to see her for the last time, but I saw the pattern at work later, and I can only, to finish her story, tell about the others and Paragraph Eleven.

For two months after my posting from initial training, I was in administration at RAF Turnbull St. Justin in Wiltshire—"Admin," the mixture of housekeeping and discipline that ran WAAF lives in the service. Paragraph Eleven was the paragraph in King's Regulations which dealt with release from the women's forces because of pregnancy. The number had replaced the word, as if even the fact of pregnancy had, in the language of authority, to be controlled by service language.

But in 1942, with all of Britain thrown together—male and female—by conscription, that imposition, like so many of the rules, was arid, ineffectual, too far from reality to be anything but a sort of "cleaning up" after the facts of wartime life. Authority forced humanity back into the fields, as if the lusty lives of the eighteenth century were still going on undisturbed, in secret, underground.

At RAF Turnbull St. Justin, I, the only American among two thousand British airmen and women, watched out of the billet window after lights-out as the WAAF officers inspected with blackout flashlights the crannies and secret places of the station. I could see them trudging along in the darkness, dim fireflies in the cold night, the dark deeds they sought out long since done in the light, the WAAF comfortable in their cots.

In the Admin office, I hauled coal for the sergeants, cleaned the floors, filled in the tan paper forms, which seemed to be the only contact with life going on somewhere else, like the old mole. At first, hamstrung between authority and reality, I was racked by these glimpses and whispers, but I, too, was slowly learning

to live secretly, without being destroyed by blind obedience—or caught. I knew authority too well and hated it
too much, but most of the others ignored it, except for
the times when it passed physically near them, when
they snapped to attention, saluted, marched, dressed
ranks, all the while making contact with their secret
eyes in a language that I, a stranger, could not understand.

Where could they go? Walking in the great west-
country fields in spring, I could hear rustling in the
winter haystacks, giggling and then silence, the burrow-
ing out of sight of shy animals. In the bluebell woods I
came upon bluebells crushed in the shapes of bodies. In
the abandoned concrete air-raid shelters, where drifts of
sodden leaves kept the smell of old rain, they found a
privacy more important than the damp and the darkness, took onto the concrete benches a human need too
great to be damped out.

In the Admin office we sat, our collars clean, our
uniforms pressed as an example to the others, and
waited for the results. I grew to love the brave, the
tough, the proud. They could be recognized by their
clothes first, the high pompadours grown back after initial training so that their WAAF caps sat at an angle
on the backs of their heads, defying gravity as their
owners defied authority, by clinging to just enough of
the rule to get by. I see them as one girl, slowly grinning, cap off with a grab, standing straight, with a kind
of ease just within the stance demanded by the sergeant
so that she could not snap "stand up," but had to sit
and wait.

"I'm 'aht."

The sergeant's scrawny hand reached for the tan paper; all lecturing stopped in the face of that easy triumph
of natural insolence, saying, "Paragraph Eleven?"

They usually were pregnant. The others, blackmail-
ing compassion from the gentle by their blind fear,
aroused fury and lecturing by the special breed of Admin NCO's, as if they were dedicated to stamping out
sex, at least in the weak, while the girl cringed within

her uniform sobbing, "It was me first toime. 'E's going to marry me."

As often as not, fear had driven them there, as to a confessional; and, found not to be "in the family way" at all, they would slink back to their jobs amid the derisive jeers of the others. The first of these that I saw, a little brown-faced, dumb girl, stood there receiving verbal blows as if the sergeant's sergeant-self were quarreling with her woman-self over her head; she waited, stunned, squat and heavy on the floor, dim and tangled in her trouble. I interceded, finding it unbearable, and asked if I could take her into the village to buy civilian clothes for her to marry in, to retrieve just a few faggots of respectability and kindness from the fires being heaped upon her.

Something flicked behind her eyes and she whimpered, "I've no coupons," in a sly Manchester voice on the scrounge.

"I have," I told the sergeant—me, lady bountiful with the valuable clothing coupons, my trunk full of American clothes in London.

How we got the few pounds together to buy her wedding dress I can't remember, but we did go into Turnbull St. Justin that day, rattling along in the back of an RAF van, the girl's mute, square, north-country face at first still with her trouble, not looking at me or answering, while I, leaning forward, clutching the tailgate of the grumbling van, tried to pour light into her, to make at least a parody of a wedding day for her, pumping her up with hope, forcing on her all the kindesss I would have prayed for in the situation. She, gradually thawing, took the whole thing for granted with a spaniel softening, as if I had been scratching her ears.

We bought a blue dress, a blue coat and useless blue sandals—not quite the same blue, but all there was in Turnbull St. Justin. They looked sleazy. The shoes, made of paper and paint, had two days of life in them—but they were new, and, for a minute before the small mirror, she looked pretty.

Then she, with her wartime parcels of thin brown pa-

per in her lap, was at last as fooled as I was, the happy
ending induced, when we got back to the station. A
scrawny young red-headed airman (I knew his mates
called him Ginger) sat desolate on the guardroom stoop
waiting for us, his head between his thin knees. When
he got up, I saw that he was no taller than she was. We
struggled out of the back of the van. He said only,
" 'Ere," in a heavy Somerset country growl and took
her parcels while she got herself down to the road.
They didn't look at each other.

That night, free of us all, the wedding couple faced
their problem in their own way. They got drunk and
shed the blows of authority and, what must have been
as hard to bear, the imposition of my demanded happy
ending. They sold the blue coat back to the shop, drank
the proceeds and fell in a muddy field, back, probably,
to the scene of their consummation. There, in the dawn,
they were found by a farmer and brought in to the station.

The little airwoman was marched into the Admin office under close arrest. The farmer had covered her
with an old musty black raincoat which fell nearly to
the floor around her. Under it, when the sergeant
stripped it off her as if she were a doll, her wedding
dress was torn and caked with mud. The blue sandals
were in shreds on her bare feet. She stood, shivering
with cold, looking as if she had been left out too long in
the rain, between two towering female MP's. They
marched in a ludicrous military line in to the WAAF
commanding officer. The door shut behind them.

A WAAF officer, one of the few I remember with
affection, stopped beside a chair, where I had sunk
down close to the stove, still staring at the closed door.
She was a blond girl who kept flowers on her desk and
always had a strand of hair straying below her attempt
at a neat roll below her cap.

She said, "You can't let them tear you to pieces.
They nearly did. . . . I thought when I got some
power . . . oh, you know, you have to forget them,
each one, I mean. It's the only way to get on."

I had got to my feet. I said, "Ma'am," which was the demanded answer for an officer when there was nothing to say.

"Don't worry, my dear," she said in the kind, secure voice of the true convert, "here's something that will help you. I'll pass it on to you each week when I've finished." She handed me a folded tract.

It was the *New Statesman and Nation,* the first copy I ever saw.

A few days later I saw the little Manchester airwoman scrubbing the cookhouse floor on WAAF jankers (punishment). She grinned and said, "I got twenty-eight days, and it weren't nuffink but a flippin' false alarm. I awsk you!" She didn't mention the sandals or the marriage.

In the pub, Tina's young officer had long since run out of things to joke about. It was two o'clock. I heard the woman call, "Tahme please," from behind her shut door, and I stood up to leave.

As I waited for the bus, I could see Tina and her man, walking slowly away down the village street.

It was our last Saturday at the initial training unit. The "passing-out" parade was over. We already had our postings to permanent stations—the five friends split apart, never to see each other again. Viv and I spent the afternoon in the ritual washing, pressing, bathing, changing of underwear after a week. For three weeks, taking on the habits of the others, I had been warmer, healthier, more obscene, more relaxed; but Viv was stiff that day with preparation and nervousness. There was to be a dance at the gym, and Viv had never been to what she called "a proper party." She washed the collar and cuffs of her best shirt and put her short hair in pins. All the time, with her worried face pushed close to the dim mirror in the ablutions, she kept asking troublesome questions—what you did, where you stood, did you ask the boys or did they ask you—and then adding that it didn't matter anyway because she couldn't dance as she put another smudge of rouge on her yellow cheeks.

The gym at RAF Hereford had been decorated with a few colored streamers. They had lost much of their color, and they looked thin and lost hanging from the high steel rafters in the large, blank space. On the stage at the end of the floor a four-piece band was playing with that peculiar solemn undercurrent of *thunk-thunk* rhythm that already sounded like the tread of feet though the floor was still empty. The WAAF sat straight in their chairs. I thought the waiting would go on forever while the band pumped out "Jealousy" slowly into the space.

Then a couple began, then another, until there were twenty or so couples, tiny under the steel vaulting, in a solemn directional tango march around the room. They reversed as if to an order, all the circle of the dancers moving in the opposite direction, not speaking to each other, concentrating on the sound of their feet.

The band played "The Beer Barrel Polka," and I heard the faint sigh of people beginning to sing. It grew louder. The directional circle went faster. I heard Viv breathe a delighted "Coo!" The party finally crossed the line from solemnity to take on a sense of violence. There are nations who dance for love or for ecstasy, but the people of the British Isles dance for war. They pass from an almost religious solemnity to battle in their northern pleasure; the heaviness of their steady feet (they dance from the knee down) erupts into an awkward wildness.

The band began to play "Run Rabbit Run Rabbit Run Run Run." Long lines of Air-Force-blue swept by, kicking, shouting, in chargelike waves—still directional—around and around the floor. Someone grabbed my arm and pulled me into one of the lines. It was a cockney from the hut. An airman joined on the outside. Sixteen of us in a line, our arms crisscrossed behind each other's backs to hold us up while we plunged, cracked the whip, *run rabbit run rabbit run run run,* making the vast sound of a tribal war stomp.

As we charged by, I glimpsed Viv sitting as straight as a duenna, smiling so that her new red mouth stretched clownlike across her face. She winked. She had finally seen me into the WAAF and she was giving up her duty.

The next day we were sent on leave, then to our separate posting. I was never to see the communal riot or sense the sheer hard battle joy again, for the Royal Air Force had a special problem. Airmen and airwomen were posted by jobs, separately, as if the training units were some great employment agency. We were never in flights again, as the aircrews were, or in companies, as in the Army, where a corps' pride could develop. It showed even in the language—one was "attached" to a station, each new place approached without knowing a soul, so that to be posted off your station was a thing to be feared and in it was a vague sense of punishment. Such isolation among the vast majority of the ground crews bred an unseen poisoned miasma, secret beneath the structure as sex was secret to authority. From time to time it reached the point of bursting forth.

Chapter 4

It took three changes to get from Hereford to Turnbull St. Justin. The trains got smaller each time. Finally I stood on the platform at Turnbull St. Justin and watched the smallest of all, the train to take you nowhere, disappear, my kitbag leaning against my leg, not knowing or caring at that little point how to get out to RAF Turnbull St. Justin. Farther down the platform an RAF officer was looking up the narrow street from the station. He didn't yet fit his uniform. It still carefully fitted him. His wings were new. He seemed as isolated as I felt. The inevitable van drew into the empty parking lot and swung around. It was driven by a WAAF in battle dress.

We were put into the back to be delivered. All along the road winding away behind us the trees were lush even in winter, the blue-green of Gainsborough in the misty light. We both stared at where we'd been, not saying a word. I finally said, "It's lovely."

"Unh?"

"The trees—green in winter . . ."

"It's *ivy.*" His face and voice warmed into anger from his mild stupor. "It's bloody ivy. A bloody blight. Parasite."

For the rest of the way to the station I got a lecture on the dangers of ivy to England. The pilot officer had been a horticulturist.

I said no more about the trees.

We could hear the Oxfords filling the air with that incessant machine buzz which substituted for silence on the station.

RAF Turnbull St. Justin lay out, aurally and physically, in a great circle whose central concentration was the aircraft itself. It was the reason we were there, and the nearer the airman was to his machine, the better was his morale, the more understandable his reason for being.

The rest of RAF Turnbull St. Justin was like the stations I had seen before—flat buildings under a leaden sky, humped oval corrugated-iron backs of Nissen huts. But at its center, the blasted space of the air field blotted out the old Cotswold grazing land in a vast square, crisscrossed by long runways. Huddled near the space, the huge hangars loomed above a few yellow Oxfords, nesting like birds. In the distance, above the other buildings, I could see the top of the flying control tower. It was built like a functional Puritan square, jutting up blindly, covered with brown and green undulations of camouflage, impotent against its unnatural shape.

I first noticed the connection between morale and the machines in the girls who came into the Admin office. Those in touch with them, the mechanics, the "met" girls, the signals operators, carried in with them a verve, a dash from nearer the center. The commanding officer at Turnbull St. Justin recognized this and decided to raise morale by taking the WAAF up for rides. He filled an Anson with WAAF cooks and flew them around the county. They were all sick. It seemed fair. They spent most of their time making us sick.

Those nearer the center suffered the rest of us as a dim necessity; the other women on the station fanned out in a sort of hierarchy of loss. The hierarchy worked on the stations themselves, from "ops"—the operational stations—through the various training commands down to the initial training units.

So when a call for volunteers to signals came into the Admin office, I volunteered, giving up the honor I was supposed to be waiting for, that of being sent into officer's training as an Admin officer. I had already realized that such officers were chosen not for specific skills, but for a mystic hangover from a distant peacetime—a quality called officermaterial, which usually meant that one's voice was careful, one's bearing "genteel," that one was, at least in form, a "lady"—all of which qualities I was trying to buff off as quickly as possible, like a useless and hampering prehensile tail, unneeded and awkward in the world I was trying to live in. Admin tended to gather together the self-conscious, the reactive, the snobs. Good officers slipped through, in spite of their qualifications, their qualities a mixture of security and strictness and grace.

I could see myself giving the sex lecture, meting out punishments I had no stomach for, dealing with a small army of "Paragraph Elevens." I was drawn away from that hard and human job, seduced toward the center— the machines.

The radio-telephone, (R/T) operators sat in the flying control tower connected to the air, human elements like fuse wires, earphones on, plugged into small Marconi transmitter-receiver crystal sets, transmitting orders from the flying control officer, receiving in turn the pilot's recognitions of the ground, complaints, questions, sometimes jokes—all in the terse cut-word code of the RAF, monosyllabic, easy to call, quick to understand, sometimes chosen with the justice of poetry.

In our ears there was a perpetual grumbling of pilots calling to each other thinly down a long sound tunnel of distance. Over it all, striking at the fuse wires, the human element, German jamming was a curtain through which we listened, an undulating carrier wave, maddening and incessant, its efficiency defeating itself for a while because after a few weeks it, like the rumble of the planes, became a part of silence, staying insidiously always in our ears on and off the set, as if it were lodged in our brains, a small, monstrous parody of the hum of the world. To think about it after so long is to hear it again, incessant, like conscience; it has, once heard long enough, sacred a place in one's brain. As with everything else, the loudness of signals heard was categorized into "strengths"—strength 5 (loud and clear) was the loudest; strength 1 was the faintest.

On eight-hour duty we learned to point our concentrated hearing through jamming at strength 3 or 4 like bird dogs to the tiny strength-1 sounds beyond it, answering, transmitting or receiving the clipped English without passion or person or intonation beyond the code sounds themselves, pencils flying through the logbooks before us, logging each fragment of sound, all as impersonal as the color of the station, hearing always through the jamming and the pinpoints of dialogue the urged rumbling of the planes.

Because of this demanded impersonality I had to learn to speak the English of the RAF in one day. The pilots, wary anyway, senses poised in the air, had no time to understand a soft, new voice; annoyed, they called back, clipped out, "Hello, Nemo. Hello, Nemo [code name for the unknown]. Re-peat. Re-peat."

I learned to speak in character, "Helleau, *Covey Ninah Fife*. Helleau, *Covey Ninah Fife.*"

I cannot remember the call sign for the central tower at RAF Turnbull St. Justin, but I remember the call signs for the Oxfords—covey—and for one Oxford—*Covey Ninah Fife*—because I have failed in forgetting.

Covey Ninah Fife was an airplane, and I remember its name though the name of my partner on duty, with whom I shared a room and a watch for months, has been forgotten; for our point of concentration and contact, our preoccupation, was the machine, which had an insane simplicity because we used human terms. We serviced the planes, called to them, lost them (in the cold, calm language of the BBC, "Eight of our aircraft are missing," oh, misplaced, their servant airmen inside, sometimes hosed out.) As are all vessels made by man, all carriers, the planes were called "her"; often they were tagged with women's names—cared for, placated, their caprices noticed, and bragged about. *Covey Ninah Fife* was like an impatient, selfish, pouting, demanding woman.

On duty in the daylight, through the wide window which covered nearly the whole of the wall of the signals room, we could see the planes we spoke to coming in to land through the white space above the airdrome. Sometimes on bright days when there was promise in the air, they buzzed the control tower in an excess of freedom. When the flying control officer tried to find out their names to report them, we in contact were suddenly struck a little deaf, unable to hear their call signs.

On those days, coming off duty and out into the sun, into the more immediate roaring of the planes taking off and landing, I would wander down toward the briefing room, drawn toward the machines at work, hoping for the illegal invitation that made my heart flip over and my adrenalin surge.

There the newly graduated pilots, with their shiny embroidered wings, not yet dulled by time and service, waited to fly for pleasure, as boys in love with the planes. None of the student pilots had "tasted" combat, much less been sickened and surfeited. The few instructors I flew with had. Their handling of the machines was calmer, controlled. They knew what they were dealing with and flew warily. The ones who had survived were sad, careful men in their twenties, stripped of arrogance, their uniforms no longer costumes but utilitarian, as rubbed down as their wings and their faces. The student pilots still flirted and called out as I came toward the briefing room, "Want to go for a flip?"

Then I ran toward Equipment for a parachute and ran back, the chute flopping against my legs, the webbing criss-crossed to a metal disk at my breastbone, and climbed into the Oxford, the Miles Magister, the Tiger Club—whatever plane was warming up. Those functional wartime planes uninsulated by upholstery, soft voices, ignorance, were as maneuverable as fine horses. I watched the stick move forward and the ground drop away from us.

England became then, in minutes, an undulating patchwork quilt. Poppies below us, in their season, made some of the fields red, some yellow, some green with white doll houses, and the ancient bones of Cotswold outcroppings, and the gray ruins turned away below us under the free sky. There was no fear, no gravity. We flew, and often, looking up to see familiar abbey ruins as landmarks directly above us, our bodies lunging against the seat belts, our senses accepted the circular vision of the earth.

We went on low-flying exercises, jumping hedges and copses with the greatest sense of speed there can be because the motion was in closest contrast to the steady, known earth. The obstacles whipped behind us as we passed over them low enough to see a steady slipstream of cows bolting and farmers swearing, to see the separation of the grass, the dangerous closeness of the plane to its tossing black shadow.

There was never a more egocentric experience of control than having, with new Phaeton power, the sense that the earth was turning, rolling toward the sky at one's command; still within the plane, one watched, quietly, fingertips as alert as brains, the close ground flow, almost touching-close. Aircraft were then instruments of the arrogance authority tried to curb, of an experience, undigested and unprepared for, of simplicity and power in frames often too frail for it. If I, stealing "flips," was having that experience, so was Tina's pilot officer, taking power into his dangerous mind, and so were the Luftwaffe, so were the other romantics— some sick souls never to grow beyond it, as a first love is sought over and over, more parodied each time. Sometimes, in me, that arrogance would reach the ground for a few minutes after we touched down as I lugged the parachute back to Equipment, and I, still airborne, walked lightly away, forgetting where I was until the voice of an officer would intrude and snap, "Airwoman, step back ten paces and salute."

The day divided itself for the R/T operators into two worlds—that on the set and that off the set. There were two constant watches—the station watch and, even more important and less used, the Darky watch, which blanketed the whole of England with overlapping limited areas of open and waiting reception. On each station, a limited-area Marconi transmitter-receiver was set to the same wavelength, each covering a small area of the open air around its station. It was the safety watch—for the lost planes, those with wounded aboard or crippled wings or knocked-out engines. Whenever a plane needed to come down at the nearest field, the call went out somewhere over England, "Hello, Darky. Hello, Darky," and the answer came, beamed from the nearest sets, "Hello, Nemo. Hello, Nemo," to ask for their identifying call sign. Because of the limited areas of sound around each set, the loudest call came from the nearest field, and the plane would swerve toward the strongest voice.

Sometimes we sat on Darky watch for weeks, waiting until, in the distance, a voice would come ghostlike through the jamming, "Hello, Darky. Hello, Darky," and we would call out safety to the unknown, "Hello, Nemo. Hello, Nemo."

One night an American voice came through at strength 1, weak, far away, "Hello, Darky, where the hell are we?" a lost thin whisper. From the overlapping answers, the radio operator in the plane sorted out the faint American lilt left in my disciplined voice. The plane flew toward it like a homing pigeon and landed, and a crew of fourteen homesick airmen from a Flying Fortress piled into the control tower to find the American girl.

The flying control officer was furious at the roar of life breaking into the silence of his night watch. He kept complaining that they had eaten all the eggs in the officers' mess.

On both watches the closeness to the air, to the machine, affected the operators. Some, uninterested in the connections with the air, made the flying control officer the keeper of their duty. When he was gone, responsibility went with him, and they turned down the sets to protect their brains from the jamming, got out knitting or books, unscrewed the "AC's" (batteries) to drop acid on their stockings so they could turn them in to Equipment for new ones.

Flying exercises kept us keyed to the sets and blotted out time with quick, concentrated work. Scrounging flips made me resurge afterward as if I had gone to a well of action, and I found a reason for being there, tied to the earphones. In the vast periods of boredom between, when only jamming could be heard, it was hard for the hand not to reach forward to turn the set down, not to recede from it into the dead areas of animal waiting, waiting for the confinement of the closed signals room, the connection by wavelength, even the sense of floating displacement in the state of war itself to be over.

Only having sought the air, and having heard, loosened in that space, the weak, thin connection with the control tower, stable through the crackling, diffused sound, kept me listening through the months, until there was no chronology of time, only place and the set, waiting before it for the always expected call.

That was the color of day, for day and night, on the set, were split apart by the color against the window. At night the blackout curtain cut us off from sight, and we waited within it through the lonely stretching of the hours toward morning. Time ceased altogether, and only those on their watches were awake in England, isolated at live points in the dark.

I sensed the feel, the taste, the smell of space that year in those expanded nights, the other operator nodding, almost asleep, talk long since having ceased; there were no words—only the expansion of the brain and fatigue, dissolving unknowingly into trance. The notes which from long habit I wrote down on any scrap of paper and stuffed into my tunic pocket had, at the time of writing, the certainty of answers; yet later, as in dream answers, they made no sense. They were the only notes I kept of my whole experience in the WAAF, but when I found them later they meant nothing. They had been dredged deep from my unconscious as I floated in night. Once I had written, "We cannot live without love any longer." And again, "The contact is from mast light to mast light to aerial to mast light." Only the crumpled wartime paper, torn from an RAF issue notebook—not the words—brought back the smell, the cold, the space of the night.

We knew that beyond us in the darkness there was nothing, and we floated high in it, in that room; there was no ground, only darkness until the nights of night-flying exercises, when the darkness came alive with sound channeled into our ears.

On those nights we knew that the flare path was stretched away, dimly pinpointing the station in the dark, the faint blue lines of light shaped into a distant funnel for the planes: tiny, confident guide points isolated in an infinite blackout. The winking red eye of the Aldis lamp would be signaling at the flare path's end by the hand of some ground-crew airman huddled in the darkness of the air field, flashing at the planes as they swooped down through the blackness.

We watched at the same time by listening; urgent, concentrated, seeing nothing but the confines of the room and the logbooks, making of those two elements and the pushing roar of the planes a whole vision of the flyers and the night.

The dark could be controlled, but not the yellow mist

which had risen to cover and mute the ancient grazing
land for as long as the Celts had run their sheep there
and which, from time to time, quickly and silently blotted out RAF Turnbull St. Justin and left us calling and
calling impotently through the soft damp blankets of
fog.

Because of the quickness of these rising mists, RAF
Turnbull St. Justin was known in the language of the
RAF as Clamp Hill.

We were told one evening at six o'clock that the ceiling was high enough for night-flying exercises. I saw
the first star in the purple sky as I pulled the blackout
curtain and we settled into our seats. The flying control
officer came in from time to time to stand behind us
and talk a little, as he tended to do when we knew there
would be the relief of night flying from the monotony
of the most disliked watch of all—the four to twelve—
when we were aware of the others wandering out to the
pubs, going to the "flicks" on the station, finding each
other in the lowering purple evening after duty was
over.

With the visibility infinite, night flying began about
eight o'clock. The exercises in taking off and landing
we called circuits and bumps. From the flying control
officer through us to the planes, the orders clipped out,
"Hello, *Covey Eight Foah,* circle at Angels fife. Hello,
Covey Ninah Three, circle at Angels foah. Hello, *Covey Ninah Two,* circle at Angels two. Hello, *Covey Ninah
Fife,* pancake."

We played at control; the planes stacked, circling
safely at five, four, three thousand feet, waiting their
turn to land, switch off and refuel, take off again to join
the circuit in an easy air quadrille.

Then the clamp fell. Within minutes the ceiling
dropped to a thousand feet, to five hundred, to three
hundred, to the deck. The other R/T operator caught
my eye and whispered one word, "Flap!" Flap—panic;
we worked faster, carriers for the urgency of the flying
control officer and the planes.

There were three down safely, then four. The set was

jammed with queries, put off by our voices, "Hello, Covey Eight Three, stand by, stand by . . ."

The planes were like air sheep taking their turns at the shambles. The new pilots, their voices crackling with urgency, flew blind, the fog pressed to their windows, their dependable sensuousness in flying no longer possible.

With the concentration of his eyes pinned to the altometer as the orders came in, *Covey Ninah Fife* flew as the others did, waiting. He heard, "Hello, *Covey Ninah Fife,* circle at Angels four," watched the altometer drop to four thousand feet, calculated the feet above sea level at RAF Turnbull St. Justin as he breathed, slipped his eye to the turn indicator, depending on the balanced bubble of the level, the horizontal position of the tiny red plane at the artificial horizon, as if he were flying it instead of some six thousand pounds of machine; plotting the place of the plane in the darkness, picturing the wings inclining through the swirling darkness to a ground level which could not be seen, but would be felt when, calculations correct, *Covey Ninah Fife* touched down, the jolt of her wheels on the ground the only indication of the agreement of the instruments.

At three thousand feet, *Covey Ninah Fife* reported in and was told to circle and stand by.

We brought down *Covey Eight Three,* concentrating so that we could almost feel her wheels touch and bounce.

Covey Ninah Fife called in, low on fuel. Urging the other planes to stand by, we began bringing her down, all of us, with that blind dependence on orders, instruments and the machines, all of the old dependence on senses channeled to brain and obedience.

We heard the relief in the pilot's voice when he touched down and began to taxi her, guided by the ghost point of the Aldis lamp. We brought down *Covey Ninah Three.*

Through it, *Covey Ninah Fife* had not received orders to switch off. The pilot's voice kept coming in, more and more urgent; he was unable to switch off without the order. *Covey Ninah Fife* idled in the fog, her propellers turning, her grumbling voice interrupting as the other planes called in and were guided down to the flare path, now with lit flares floating, almost invisible, in the eye-tricking, muting fog.

There were two planes still up. With the excess of care engendered by panic, thin-voiced orders went out, dropping them in turn to three, then two, then one thousand feet.

Covey Ninah Fife called in, petulant, annoyed, for orders.

"It's *Covey Ninah Fife,* sir," I told the flying control officer, as urgent as the plane.

"Christ, I thought she was down," he said, forgetting in an hour of flap each separate plane.

"She is. She came down half an hour ago."

"Then for Christ's sake tell her to sign off."

"She . . ."

Covey Eight Three called in for orders to land and reported that she was low on fuel. We were off again, guiding as carefully as if we were setting her down safely on the ground with our own hands.

As we worked mechanically within the dependable rotation, so in the darkness did the ground crews, feeling their way through the clamp to the planes, swarming over them, refueling to orders and by habit, though the planes were grounded, the fog grease-slick on their wings. It was drill leaving no room for improvisation, drill drilled in so deeply that circumstances could not change it, drill becoming animal reaction: dependable, certain habit carrying all of us through the natural caprice of the fog. No one was yet experienced enough, or brave enough, or self-reliant enough; we were dulled by training, not yet used to being relit by danger, not capable of knowing when to disobey.

I knew it was midnight by the touch of my relief on my shoulder. We changed places quickly, the earphones still on my ears as she slid into place and got her pencil in hand. I slipped the earphones from my head to hers—even as they went on, her pencil began moving. The last plane was being brought in.

I heard her say, "Hello, *Covey Ninah Fife*," as I stepped back out of the periphery of the set, the panic and the flying control officer. I put on my greatcoat, not waiting for my partner on duty, whose relief had not yet arrived. I wanted to get out of the atmosphere of urgency, to breathe, even in the thick fog and the blackout, to steal a cigarette while I waited for her so that we could guide each other back to the billet through the fog.

The hall below the control room had only the light from the opening doors of the rooms above to filter down to it. I felt the wall in the dark toward the outside door and opened it. After the blackness of the hall, the fog seemed to carry its own faint light. Somewhere beyond me, the fog obliterating any sense of distance, I could see a dim fuzz of light moving—a blackout torch. There was no sound but the grumbling of the taxiing planes.

I lit a cigarette.

Something, rolling like a football, brushed against my leg, and I reached down toward it to pick it up and give it back toward the sound of steps running toward me.

Someone yelled, "Jesus, it's a WAAF. *Get inside.*"

One of the ground crew reached for me to push me back into the hallway before I saw him. He swept me inside with a flying tackle. For a second we clung together like lovers so that we wouldn't fall. He switched on his torch and his face rose out of the hall darkness above it. His head seemed disembodied in the dark.

"He got up on the wing to refuel *Covey Ninah Fife*," the airman said, not to me, not to anybody. "He slipped on the wing. He slipped in the fog on the wing. The prop was still going. He last his head."

For a second I thought he meant panic, then I knew what he meant and I knew what had bounded past my leg and I was sick on the floor.

Covey Ninah Fife had not received her orders to switch off.

Survival

There are fragments of recall, like lights, to explain the rest. This is a fragment.

It was when the V-1's stopped that they killed. So long as the motorcycle rumble went on in the air above us we were safe. When it cut, the V-1 either plunged or glided.

I walked along the street in Kensington, where the dampness seeped in dark patches on the dirty pavement. I carried a brown-paper parcel. It was very still because it was four o'clock in the afternoon, and not time yet for movement, certainly not time. I heard a motorcycle in the air, low above the houses, riding nearer and nearer over the street. A car drove to the side of the street and stopped. There were three of us, two people in the car, I on the pavement. The sound tore the Kensington air. It stopped. There was complete silence. I folded toward the pavement, as slow as dreaming. The bag splayed out from my hand and hit the palings of an area-way. It spurted cigarettes and cold cream. Face down on the pavement, my head cushioned in my arms against blast, in the position of grief, I waited. My body yearned toward the protection of the concrete. It would not let me in. The air split apart in a vast yell of sound. The pavement surged up to slap my chest. There was silence, and through me, in answer to the slap, a surge of life that had halted in the waiting. I was alive, vulnerable on the pavement. I got up and gathered the contents of my broken bag. The car across the street started out again. I walked on. Behind me the sounds of rescue turned into a mews. I smelled the arid flying rubble of the burst houses, but I did not look back. We did not gape at the death of other people. There was a politeness. I picked up a hot piece of shrapnel with my handkerchief. I was in the relief of life. After such recognitions, to be alive is to bear a gift, a sense of gentleness, never a right. Through the war one felt it given, over and over, as a gift.

Chapter 5

As RAF Turnbull St. Justin's great square was imposed on the fields, cutting across the old winding lanes, ignoring the rise and fall of the land, so we in uniform—in our uniformity—were imposed, star patterned, on the villages surrounding the station, changing them so that they had an air of desertion about them, an atmosphere of neglect. The villagers were outnumbered by the airmen; a new language was heard in the streets and the hard growl of the few RAF cars rumbled through them. Always there were the roar of the planes overhead, the new service graves in the ancient churchyards, the constant silent traffic of the issue bicycles.

The tiny village of St. Justin-over-Water was eight miles from the central station. I first knew it by ear, by the interfering casual blur of voices on the R/T, from our satellite station near the village. I could hear ease in the voices farther away from authority's gravity.

So, one day in the late spring, off duty, I rode my issue bicycle first along the wide road, then into the smaller lanes that separated the fields, with their new shoots of grain, and past the hedges blooming with pale pink wild roses that sweetened the warm air. I cycled faster and faster, all alone, with that rare sense of freedom that being alone and having no plans and being in the sun could give then.

There was a new quality to the freedom that made that day unlike the others. For the first time, I sensed an irresponsibility, an ease of letting go. My uniform was issue, my bicycle was issue. I was utterly without worry about where my food was coming from. As long as I did what I was told, kept silence and remained acquiescent, I had freedom from decision, freedom from want, freedom from anxiety for survival. That, too, seemed out of my hands—the decision of an abstract, an order from "above." For a few minutes as the rose hedges swept past me, I felt an almost mystic contentment.

Then, even in the sun, cold fright caught me and I peddled faster, as if I could ride away from the space of that feeling. I had experienced the final negative freedom, that of the slave, but it was only a sense, a whiff of fear. I did not reason, only rode out of it between the hedged fields toward the village.

St. Justin-over-Water lay in a deep-cut valley below the level of the surrounding sun haze. I could see its roofs, sunken beside a tiny stream, a few houses, a church; all were stone, as if they had not been built but had thrust up out of the soil by the water on their own. They looked as peaceful as a dream, and I, catching the peace, stopped the bicycle, lurched aside, one foot on the road, and watched from high above the village down the long steep deserted road that curved into the only street. Nothing moved. I could hear the birds and hear, rather than feel, a faint breeze above me in the trees lining the road. So I let go and let the bicycle drift down the hill, silent as dream movement. Faster and faster, unconsidered, I flew down toward the village, through its street, past the cottages, past the pub, past the church, through flashes of gray stone and green and, on a stone wall by the pub, a flash of Air-Force blue. I came to a stop at the end of the village and left my bicycle against the stone wall which went down the length of the street by the water.

At first I thought it was deserted, then I realized that war had seeped into rather than overlain St. Justin-over-Water. Age had formed the green lichen on the wall and on the stone bridge that crossed the water. Below the bridge I could see lazy trout, and I felt, in my relief after the station, as lazy and wandering as the fish, in that world of service, relieved, reprieved for a little while from duty. But in the churchyard, wartime neglect crawled over the untended graves; the unmown grass, studded with wild flowers, was high around the stones, so long there that, like the village, they seemed outcroppings of, not impositions on, the grass.

At the small manor house built of the same stone, the grass grew high between the great flat stones of the courtyard. A stone urn had been pushed over so long before that grass and weeds grew out of its spewn dirt. Above the weeds of the garden, the rose trees had outgrown their disciplined wiring and let their tendrils hang like escaped tresses of hair covered with roses. Through the manor house window I saw the service blackout curtains in the nearly empty drawing room and the dull floor where once the sun had dusted across the high polish and set it gleaming. Now it was scrubbed, dead wood. The inevitable flotsam of service gear lay near an open door. I knew at once that the manor house was not deserted, but was a billet. It reflected that part of war which was a kind of functional neglect, the neglect of those requisitioned houses lived in and loved for so long now being used without being looked at or cared for or tended. The cots, the deal tables, were imposed on their emptiness, never a part of them.

What had seemed desertion but was neglect made me turn away from the house, too sad even to pick one of the forgotten roses. Besides, that inculcated fear of getting caught surged up and, for a minute, until I was outside the gate again, destroyed the tenuous sense of freedom I had found. There was already waiting behind my free movement a sense of doing wrong, of breaking some rule I didn't know existed. I had learned, except in moments of release, to walk carefully, to inhibit, to remain safely unnoticed—a learned sick mildness of soul.

So, walking back along the street by the stone wall, the moment over, I was caught again, hardly noticing the lovely cottages which opened directly off it. Their wooden doors were streaked and dull, but there had been bright paint on them, in contrast to the stone, now turning pink in the late afternoon sun.

Someone said, "You ought to watch it. You could kill yourself, going that fast."

I had forgotten the free descent into the village.

Two sergeant pilots sat on the wall. Their uniforms were the old gray-blue of long service. They both had quiet faces. I thought at first that it was the afternoon. Then I saw that they both had service ribbons and, on the pocket flaps of their battle dress, tiny silver Maltese crosses.

The first, who was the spokesman, introduced himself as Sergeant Nightingale. They both sounded so at ease, so familiar, unfamiliarity having somehow worn away from their faces and their uniforms, that it seemed simple to pull myself up and sit on the wall beside them.

In my ignorance, I thought at first that they might be Maltese, because of the crosses, and I wondered at their suntanned, thin, tired, but very English faces and their voices. Then I remembered Malta. For some reason, not wanting to look just then at their faces, I concentrated on Sergeant Nightingale's hands as we sat in the last of the sunlight giving back and forth remarks at the surface of our minds, remarks that meant nothing, but kept us in a kind of easy contact. Those hands that clutched the stone wall as if, at any minute, Sergeant Nightingale were preparing to vault off it and run away up the street had been put to use to survive service in Malta, one of the worst services in the war. They were experienced hands. Even old-young Sergeant Nightingale's voice, a little muted without his knowing it, was still capable of rising in a paean of complaints, mostly about being sent back to bloody training like a bloody sprog. They had just returned and had been sent to the satellite station for a refresher course, one of the RAF methods of giving a rest to pilots who had finished a tour of duty.

They, their senses still charged to the outside capability of survival that humans can key to, had been set down, overstimulated and exhausted, in that idyllic little village to unwind slowly and realize that, for a little while, they had survived.

That realization was not spoken but, from what they said, was like blood coming back into frozen fingers, gradually and with a painful joy; it was beginning to be experienced in the soft air of the afternoon—the resurging of halted life.

We went to the pub for beer, and afterward they walked me up the long, long hill that I had flown down and made me promise to come back for a celebration in the sergeant's mess. What the celebration was about no one said, but it was because they were alive and back in England, and there wasn't anything to call such a party.

In the easy natural meeting in the afternoon we had all forgotten authority, which they had not experienced as a self-governing force that existed for its own sake, like a pall somewhere over our heads during the whole time of their active service out of England; the community of those whose lives depend on each other is as alien to imposed authority as health is to sickness.

This time I found authority acting in a feminine, comic and entirely understandable way.

We didn't know it, but the three WAAF NCO's in the Admin office were keeping the Malta pilots for themselves. A call had come into the Admin office asking for WAAF to come to their party. After much discussion lasting, I imagine, about four minutes, they decided that such an experience would be too upsetting for most of the other ranks and, after serious consideration, so as not to let the squadron of sergeant pilots down, that they would go themselves. Now, it happened that the three lady NCO's were almost parodies of everything we like to think is not true about the women's forces. They were blindly autocratic, they had all the hopes but few of the attributes of femininity and, unfortunately, they were as ugly as the wicked sisters in *Cinderella*.

Warrant Officer Boggs was brown, lean as a snake, leather covered; she flicked her whip with a sarcasm that stung as it ridiculed—from time to time soft girls got crushes on her. Sergeant Love, on the other hand, was six feet tall and weighed nearly two hundred pounds. She, the best of the lot, had inside her bulk the longing heart of a romantic. Sergeant Smerd was just five feet tall—a tiny, sadistic bundle of wire, without flesh between her skin and her bones, her eyes agate cold. She was married to a sergeant on another station and, since her way of putting me into my place was to order me to run behind her bicycle like a dog as she rode around the station, her tiny legs pumping away, I hope they didn't breed and train a child.

At any rate, the rule they made up for the occasion stated "all ranks below the rank of sergeant from RAF Turnbull St. Justin must leave the sergeant's mess at RAF St. Justin-over-Water and report back at 2100 hours on 6/8/42." It was very military. It happened to apply only to me.

They were sorry, since the party started at 2000 hours (eight o'clock), but they did allow me to cycle through the still, light summer evening with them down the lovely road to St. Justin-over-Water, to meet Sergeant Nightingale in the pub and to tell him I could not come to the party. All three of them, considering their faces and their uniforms, had on a quantity of lipstick and rouge that managed to look faintly obscene, like Tommy Trinder as Carmen Miranda at the Palladium.

We went past the hedges in a long line, WO Boggs in front, Sergeant Smerd behind her and Sergeant Love and I weaving back and forth in the rear to keep from passing them. At one point, beginning to enjoy the game, we had dropped so far behind that we could see them around a bend of the road, the solemn, low, painted head of Sergeant Smerd following the solemn, high, painted head of WO Boggs along the green hedges as if they would ride along forever on their way to stop something from happening.

We walked our bicycles down the hill into the village.

It had been bound to happen sometime—a break in the anonymity of the service. Inside the pub beside Sergeant Nightingale, his tunic unbuttoned, his legs flung out below the table, sat Wing Commander Tommy Watson, back from Malta. I had helped see him off from a short tour of duty in Washington the year before. His grin was lighting up the pub.

"Well, you did it," he said. "Bloody good."

Sooner or later I knew I had to tell Sergeant Nightingale I couldn't stay for the party. I did it sooner. The announcement raised a roar of laughter in the pub.

"It's a command," I explained.

Winco Tommy Watson said, "What's the rank of your CO?"

"She's a flight officer."

"Then that's done. I outrank her. ACW Blops, I command you to stay for the party."

It sounded terribly easy to play at it like a game, and, in touch with the Malta pilots, all that dimming cloud of indifference and imposed demand seemed to split for a minute and expose a reality that shone. We started drinking cider.

Sergeant Smerd was standing by the table, her body furious as usual, her head just above mine.

"ACW Settle, you have half an hour to report back."

"She's not going, Sergeant, I commanded her to stay." Winco Tommy Watson told her, very simply and sincerely. English country cider is very strong.

"Yes, sir." She stepped back and saluted.

"I'm the CO of this bloody squadron," he explained to us after she had gone.

At 2100 hours, Sergeant Nightingale, with one arm guiding my bicycle and the other around me, and Winco Tommy Watson on the other side, also with his arm across my back, and I, in the middle, trod lightly up the hill, sharing the sense of levitation in the twilight of the double summer time, which was coloring the stone houses nearly gold and letting the first cold of the evening creep up from the tiny trout stream. It smelled of dews and damps and roses and evening and new grass and cider. All along the road ahead and behind, the pilots from Malta were wandering out of the pub and up the evening street in twos and threes toward the mess up the hill away from the sunken village. WO Boggs and Sergeant Love had found sergeant pilots to push their bicycles. Sergeant Love looked blissful.

At the top of the hill there were two roads. Straight ahead was the road back to my billet, to signing in, to acquiescing. To the left went the road to the sergeant's mess. I slowed down.

"Come on, I'll call your CO and explain," Winco Tommy Watson told me and Sergeant Nightingale. "I'm sure she's a good type. Most of those types good types."

We went on to the left. It had hardly been a pause. We were singing then, very quietly to match the evening, "She wheeled a wheelbarrow, through streets broad and narrow, singing 'cockles and mussels, alive, alive-O'," trying to harmonize. Along behind us the loud sound of "Roll me over in the clover" put us off key, and we started again carefully, standing still in the road to put our heads together and hum the key.

The sergeant's mess of RAF St. Justin-over-Water, was a large Nissen hut, or rather two, set at right angles to each other. Somebody had fixed the phonograph (mess phonographs were easily broken), and as we piled into the mess, it was grinding out the inevitable "Jealousy." Sergeant Nightingale and I, Sergeant Love and her pilot, even WO Boggs and hers, marched solemnly around the floor, beginning the party. Wing Commander Watson had disappeared.

That was in one room of the double Nissen hut. In the front room, noise was drowning out "Jealousy." The first keg of cider had been broached. A far more interesting rhythm was rising—the rhythm of singing and crashing about. Sergeant Nightingale and I drifted toward the noise. WO Boggs and Sergeant Love went on being pushed around the otherwise deserted floor. Sergeant Smerd, the little wasp, was nowhere to be seen.

Later the pilots were draped around the deal tables, the half-broken chairs, the concrete floor like flung banners. Winco Tommy Watson sat at the center table, Sergeant Nightingale and I beside him. He kept explaining that he had tried to call my CO, but hadn't been able to reach her. But it was all all right. Everything was fine. They explained to me carefully the merits of the Beau—the Beaufighter.

Sergeant Nightingale and I went out to get air, still discussing the merits of the Beau. Outside the door of the mess, the air refused to hold us up. We settled to the ground and rested there, still discussing the Beau. Somewhere above us, Sergeant Smerd appeared again, tall, for once, in the night.

"ACW Settle, it's time you went home," she told me.

I told her where to put something.

From someplace in the dark, also at ground level, Sergeant Love's voice called, "Bleeding hell, can't you ever stop, Smerd?"

The interruption over, Sergeant Nightingale and I went on discussing the Beau, and life, in beautiful abstractions. From Sergeant Love's part of the grass came silence, punctuated by grunts and sighs. But Sergeant Nightingale and I lay belly down as we had fallen on the walk, holding hands, needing talk more than sex. We had found each other at last, and we understood everything.

Somewhere in the night space, the front room was quiet. Sergeants were asleep over the chairs and the floor. Sergeant Nightingale, Winco Tommy Watson and I still talked—on and on and on.

"I'm frightfully sleepy," Winco Tommy Watson told us. "Would you get my car and bring it to me? I don't want to walk."

Very sensibly, we lugged several of the pilots out of the way of the wooden end of the Nissen hut. Then we went to get the CO's car, obeying his order. We drove it, quite slowly, through the end of the Nissen hut and up to the table. There wasn't enough noise to wake up the pilots. He thanked us and sank into the back of the car. Then, driving carefully because, as he explained it, he had had something to drink, Sergeant Nightingale backed the car out of the ruined end of the Mess, and we drove Winco Tommy Watson back to his billet and dumped him inside.

The Malta pilots' party was gone—asleep, disappeared, celebrated to a halt. Out in the before-dawn darkness, Sergeant Nightingale rode escort for me through the dark roads, our bicycles winding back and forth, floating along under the stars between the silent fields, England peaceful around us, no light within sight but the natural faint light of the sky. Sergeant Nightingale hit a tree and decided to leave his bicycle draped around the trunk and climb up onto a low branch and rest for a while. I left him there and went on weaving in a long bicycle dance down the road, concentrating on a poem I was chanting. "I have been to Ludlow Fair, and left my necktie anywhere . . ." I called it out to the darkness and kept time with my bicycle. It was the right poem for the faint, floating journey. I could only remember two lines of it. That didn't matter either.

Eight miles later, with great care as the first wisp of dawn came into the billet windows over the sleeping WAAF in their cots, I tiptoed through the room and got myself to bed.

When I woke up, it was bright daylight and I was cider sick. Over me stood Sergeant Smerd.

"ACW Settle," she recited to the wall over my enormous head, "you are under close arrest. Failure to obey orders. Failure to appear on parade. Insubordination to a noncommissioned officer."

I vaguely remembered telling her and, through her, all the rest of the mean-eyed jailors where to put it and even what it was. I sighed.

Sergeant Smerd made me quick-march behind her bicycle all the way to the station, a mile away from the billet. At least the exercise helped to clear my head.

In the hall outside the CO's office, we formed a line. My cap was taken away. No other rank under close arrest was allowed any loose gear with which he, she, it could strike an officer. After two hours' sleep I couldn't have struck a fly. Because of the solemnity of the occasion and with a fine eye to the look of the thing, WO

Boggs and Sergeant Love placed me between them to march into my trial. Sergeant Smerd, far too tiny for the right picture, since WO Boggs and Sergeant Love were far taller than I was, brought up the rear. WO Boggs shouted out, "Attention" in the little hallway. I felt sick again. She made too much noise.

WO Boggs shouted, "By the ri-ight. *Quick march*."

Through the door we stamped. WO Boggs ran into a mathematical problem which almost defeated the whole military procedure, for the commanding officer had decided to set her desk at a pleasingly unsoldierly angle to the wall. WO Boggs marched us to the wall dead ahead and ordered a left turn, which left us facing the desk in a sort of pig line with me, the prisoner, entirely hidden behind Sergeant Love's broad back. Since I obviously couldn't play peek-a-boo around her while I was being tried, WO Boggs ordered another left turn. This time we halted at a flirtatious 60-degree angle to the desk. All this time the commanding officer sat waiting at attention. WO Boggs got an inspiration. "Ri-ight *wheel!*" she ordered, then *"halt!"* We finally stood, Sergeant Love to my left, WO Boggs to my right, and I, without my cap, in the middle, in front of the CO's desk. Sergeant Smerd was somewhere behind us. I could feel her—a kind of emanation of brittle bones. I wanted to congratulate WO Boggs. We had marched all over the little room.

There was a blank paper on the desk under the CO's hand. She tapped it, and I let only my eyes roll down to see what it was. She was tapping my virgin-clean crime sheet. I snapped my eyes back to stare at the wall behind her head. At attention it is impossible to look at anyone. You see them obliquely with your space-fastened military eyes.

Flight Officer Trimmingham was an ex-tennis player, a good sport and an absolutely unquestioning snob. To her a good backhand, a cultivated voice and a contempt for either abstract intelligence or woolly compassion were all a part of divine right. I'm sure she had never questioned a motive or a position in her life.

She began my trial. "Well. ACW Settle, we have been a bit of a fool, haven't we?" Having begun my trial, she finished it at once, without asking for any evidence from the sergeants. The "we" offended me. She looked incapable of folly and she certainly wasn't sharing my head.

"I don't want to dirty your crime sheet, since you're Officer-material, so let's just have one day confined to camp since it's a first offense. One day won't appear on your record. Let's be more careful in the future, shall we?"

We were dismissed. As we started wheeling around the room again, the CO said to Sergeant Smerd, almost as an afterthought, "Oh, Sergeant, you will assign punishment fatigues until seventeen hundred hours."

We finally made it again into the outer room. I was given my cap back by a furious WO Boggs. I didn't blame her. She could say nothing, but we both knew that the punishment had in no way fitted the crime. We also knew that there were more ways to mete out punishment for WAAF than were dreamed of by the "good sport" who had just dismissed us. If WO Boggs was furious, so, in fairness, was I. I had stood guard over WAAF before the same CO, seen her hand out punishment of a month confined to camp for missing a train, her athletic pseudo-man body stiff with disdain, exercising her new power as she would have exercised her muscles. As the Officer-material she spoke of, I would have given myself a month confined to camp. As an aircraftwoman second class, I was not grateful for being singled out by that undefined favortism of being "one of us." I knew I would have to pay for it.

Running along through the station toward the officer's mess behind Sergeant Smerd's bicycle while the men turned away, as they so often did, disgusted at the blatancy of much WAAF punishment, I saw Sergeant Smerd's flat back as yet another of the athletic physical jokes demanding power as its panacea and finally getting it in wartime for the first time in this generation of women in such new and awkward authority; but running along behind her, it was too hard then to arouse pity for her. That took years of retrospect. At the time, I just wished she was dead.

First, to "teach me who I was," in that perversion of class consciousness the English love and hate and for which I was so unprepared, she had me haul coal to the fireplaces of the officer's mess, while the few officers resting and reading papers in their morning off-duty hours got up and left the rooms and the mess attendant, an old regular Air Force corporal, stood fuming at the interference.

Then our little parade of two went jogging off to the back of the cookhouse, where large bins of garbage waited to be loaded onto a van. There I found an old friend, a conscientious objector who was always having his nose rubbed. We loaded garbage together, while Sergeant Smerd watched from her bicycle, enjoying the sight more than she minded the smell.

It was 1100 hours. The first off-duty airmen were coming in for dinner. The warm smell of the inside of the cookhouse, with its huge vats of hot food, mingled with the smell of the swill. That, and after effects of the cider, made me turn and lean against the cookhouse wall. My friend whispered, "Only hate can poison you," as I stood trying to stop heaving. He was a religious conchie.

Sergeant Smerd was hungry. She went off to her dinner and left me in the charge of the cookhouse corporal, with orders for me to scrub the floors for the rest of the day. That's how I remember that it was Friday. The floor was covered with fish scales, and for the rest of the day, nurtured from time to time with hot cups of the only good tea in the cookhouse—which the attendants made for themselves and shared with the "janker wallah," me—I saw the cookhouse from floor level.

I pushed a scrub brush over what seemed to be mile after mile of fish scales, through the noise of dinner, then the quiet afterward, through the preparations for tea and the smell of vats of frying fish. The scrubbing ceased to be punishment and became a job to do. The cider cleared from my head, and, gradually, I began to find a rhythm in the changing of the scrub water, the finding of a method of just so much of the floor to be done with each bucket, trying to make the damp concrete shine.

At 1600 hours I was scrubbing near one of the back windows of the cookhouse. I heard a whisper above me. There, in the window, was the contrite face of Winco Tommy Watson.

"I'm frightfully sorry," he called through the window. "I've just waked up."

An International
Misunderstanding

There was one Russian attached to the station. No one quite knew why he was there. He wandered around, looking lonely, in his brown uniform, his red collar almost invisible on his short neck, like one sad-eyed leftover from an Asiatic hoard.

One evening he asked me to go for a walk. We walked on and on, he half as tall and twice as wide as I was. We walked silently over three or four miles of fields, as if it were a job. The Puritan from the East had met the Puritan from the West, and we stamped through the pretty fields on a good utilitarian route-march for two.

Finally we stopped at a stile to rest.

"Aye wahnt you," he said, "ass wan peeg wahnts anahther."

"My *dear young man*," I said, "I am not a pig."

I left him there by the stile, wondering at the West, and marched back alone to the station.

Chapter 6

After sleeping in such isolation with so many, I wanted, on my first leave in London, to be alone, to wander, to make the contact which was made easily, without the tendrils of past and habit, without name—loose, to relax and find my own London.

I arrived from a different angle now, not from the luxury of peace, but from the west country. From the new angle there was a longer way to go. The people seemed not so much changed by the state of war as shrunk by it; they seemed to be protecting oases of comfort or stability and gave a sense of hiding and hoarding, not material things—the English were too honest for that—but habits, a way of having days, old wornout prejudices that no longer fitted the circumstances. We may look back with a mistaken nostalgia; but that is youth we miss, not the state of war—where we were shrunken, cramped in gesture, acquiring those habits which protected and hid us from some abstract force no one could name but which threatened loss and exposure.

In the first months in the service I, too, had retreated, without knowing it, into a watchful solitude—a parody of that "sweet solitude" that Emerson wanted the self-reliant to carry within themselves into the crowd. This was a retreat within the skin, a more tentative touching of outside objects without being conscious of one's lack of trust in one's betraying new environment. After the war, I saw a man in a dinner jacket walk into a restaurant and look around him, testing what he saw with his eyes, touching the scene to see if it would hold him; he moved carefully from somewhere within his clothes, taking up too little of his space. I knew at once that he had been in prison.

In the very young I saw less of this—they grew

within the conscript world—but in the civilians, in the women, surprised, stunned out of custom, it was there, carried within them, the shrinkage of old shock.

In the limbo between friends and the service, I found a room I hoped would be anonymous, to go out from it, to be able to choose. The English Speaking Union sent me to Mrs. Ethel Mead, who had the top two floors of a Kensington house. She rented rooms to nice girls whose families were "her sort" and worried about their morals. She was Anglo-Irish, with that thin, dainty gentility that went to her blood—moving slowly through her thin, shocked body and leaving her cold all the time—her face the gray of women who had stood in queues through too many biting windy days. She wore, or rather moved somewhere within, one of those heavy tweed skirts and long oatmeal cardigans that came from a whole world of common-sense uniformity but are never seen in any shop. Where to buy them is an underground secret handed around the women's institutes or the church bazaars.

My room was on the top floor. Two thin careworn sprigged hand towels and a bath towel were hung carefully on a white spindled towel rack by the hand basin. The bed back was pale green, like the bed cover. On the bedside table under a frilled, precarious lamp, a terrible little heavy brass frog sat, its mouth opened to receive ashes. As Mrs. Mead showed me around the room, her thin hands crawled carefully over the objects. It was as if her hands themselves were leaving a trail of her life over the room, as, in her apologies, she let fall the facts, hardly knowing or caring, her tired voice trailing after her. The bed, the dresser, had been in her family home in Ireland outside of Dublin, the ashtray from service in India, the hand towels from "before the war"—as if it were a place, not a time, a place she came from and wanted me to know about. Finally she paused, or rather her hand paused, slid down one of those small rickety vases that never seems to have been bought but always to have existed on the lace-trimmed runners of such dressers. "There would have been mimosa this time of year," she said vaguely. Then she took my leave ration card and left me alone until teatime.

I was caught, exhausted, in the frail, poor, haunted room. Outside, the brown misted roofscape of Kensington seemed to go on and on over miles of such pale, preserved places—no wartime neglect, but rather its opposite—a preoccupation with survival at the level of carefully patched chintz, of objects worn down by the checking caress of thin hands to see if they were still there. The only real evidence of war in the room was my own kitbag, intruding, and my shoes, heavy black utilitarian objects, which I set carefully side by side, as if I were being watched by Mrs. Mead. There was no place to sit except a delicate chair with mother-of-pearl inlay, which would have held me, but not, I was sure, the alien uniform I wore. I carefully pulled back the green cover and lay on the bed, succumbing to the twilight limbo of Kensington on a winter afternoon in an almost unbearable stretch of silence after the vast insect buzz of engines, enemy jamming and the piercing yells of service life, any one of which would have shattered the room.

I must have slept. The last thing I remember was the yawning mouth of the heavy ashtray letting the last smoke from a Woodbine trail upward. There was dim tap on the door, and a boy's voice said quietly, "Tea is ready." It was exactly four-thirty, and the hollow light outside the window had deepened.

In the living room Mrs. Mead sat behind the brittle unmatched teacups, gray slices of National bread and fragments of biscuits—the ration eked out to four fragmented meals because that was the way it had always been, she said as she handed me tea. She made no comment on my uniform or my being there, not that first day. We had tea because it was time, lowering outside toward the city night. I, too, was expected to take for granted, without comment, the fact that little Mrs. Mead was dressed in the heavy black trousers and tunic of a ARP warden.

Her fifteen-year-old son, Terence, his blond hair as frail as his growing wrists and ankles, wearing the gray uniform of some city school, withdrew behind his cup and didn't say a word.

Nobody said a word. In the silence the teacups rattled reverently in their hollow saucers.

Mrs. Mead told Terence that it was time (as it had always been) to draw the drawing-room curtains. Then she added, with a slight apologetic cough at the personal remark, "See to the bedrooms. You don't mind if he goes in, do you?"

Terence was already fastening the close-fitted blackout blinds into place and pulling the faded chintz draperies across to hide them.

"I would be grateful if you would draw your blackout curtains before you come down. You can't be expected to know . . ."

The Chinese problem of "knowing" without telling or being told was twenty times worse in England in wartime. I was so overconscious of shortages that I read the word "NOVIO," stamped on the toilet paper, as a date—November 10. The fact that it was late November didn't enter my mind. I was simply frozen with care and guilt at using two of the dated squares. Gradually, the fact that it was a trademark became evident even to me, but I saved a great deal of Mrs. Mead's toilet paper before I found out.

Mrs. Mead gathered up her tin helmet and her knitting bag to go on duty. I found out then where the cardigans came from—from ARP duty, in the shelters, at the R/T sets, waiting for the trains to come in so that thick cups of tea could be handed out to troops. All across England there was a huge net of half-finished knitting—khaki-drab, navy-blue, Air-Force blue and civilian "depot beige"—as the women waited in that stretched spacial time I knew so well for the war to end. Nostalgia has muted and softened the click of knitting needles and machinery's droning on in the quiet of that tired waiting, and the deep grunt of the guns, the sounds of singing, the hoot of sirens are jackknifed in my memory into a continuous sound, a telescoping of memory. I had forgotten the silence, not mystic but halted, as if we were all waiting in one vast depot for an interrupting train that never came but was always coming, so that nothing could be planned and carried through.

After Mrs. Mead had gone, leaving instructions littering the space of that curtained room so cut off from outside by the blackout that it could have been five hundred feet up anywhere, unconnected any longer to anything but the night it floated in, Terence and I sat, farther away from each other without her there to focus on the tea tray. He still held himself stiff in his chair, his thin hands, like his mother's, clasped together so that the knuckles were white in the blue winter skin, his knees taut against each other, his face immobile with his shy control. Only his ears, sticking beyond his flopping, damp-looking blond young hair, betrayed him; they were red with exertion, as if they carried all his curiosity, all his life at that moment.

He said, "You may smoke if you like," and took a Woodbine out of his pocket, watching me join him to see if I would join or betray. We smoked without a word, and after the ceremony was over, he took both ashtrays out. I could hear him flushing the fag-ends down the toilet. He came back and sat down in the same position, while the toilet sighed on and on.

Outside, starting low, the air-raid sirens began to fill the air with their spreading layers of sound. Terence didn't move.

"Do we go anyplace?" I had to ask.

"Oh, no, not unless we hear planes," he answered with some unconscious contempt.

The grunting of great guns began. I didn't know what they were.

He knew it. There was less space between us in the room.

"That's ack-ack in the park," he told me. "You can tell by the rhythm." There was a huge discernible pattern. "Would you like to go up on the roof?" Terence invited me politely and kept on watching me until I nodded yes. What I really wanted to do in that first warning was to run and burrow underground.

Out on the roof of the building, where before there had been only spacial blackness, we leaned on the stone railing and watched the impossible inhuman new air-scape. The black was crisscrossed by moving straight bright lines drawn by the searchlights. They waved in their own directions, as far as we could see over the city. Away in the distance across the black lake that was London, a tiny fire flowered. The ack-ack guns in the park kept up their steady rhythmic grunt. Terence touched my arm. I could just see him, a darker shadow pointing up. Above the park two searchlights had fingered through the black until they met and fixed on the tiny black bug of a plane, caught and pinned it on their fused point. The ack-ack guns redoubled their volume. The tiny object lunged and turned its way out of the trap of light and sound and was gone. The light lines wandered aimlessly, catching nothing more.

The single long note of the All Clear rose and died. At once toylike and vast, the casual night raid was over. I tried to sleep in that blackness which, when the little bedside lamp was out, permeated the strange high bedroom, its safe and usual furniture gone; there was no glow from the coke stove, no sound of sleepers, moving alive as in the barracks, only silence and pressing primordial blackness. I wondered how many people kept on sleeping in the subway stations, how many wartime love affairs were consummated to avoid that primordial pressure of black of rooms in wartime cities, exposed in war to the extreme elements of dreams—pure pressure of black, the constant silence of escape, the minuscule naked exposure to the bombs shaped and released like shit from the air, the infinite aloneness of the tiny pilot exposed in corridors of light. There was no need for dreaming. That would come later to all of us. Then, the night was truer than dreams, its motion as infinitely slow.

All the next day I wandered through the London

streets in the pale misty sun, loose and free, escaped from the night, still on leave from that new direction I had come, not ready to take up the disguise of civilian clothes, the connections with acquaintances in their little groups.

There was another problem. After paying Mrs. Mead, I had five carefully saved pounds, and I could not rescue my civilian clothes without, in that largesse people without money demand of themselves, tipping the terrifying butler who guarded the heavy double door (so high it had another mean little door imbedded in it for "everyday" use) in one of the partly inhabited houses of Carlton House Terrace, where the owning rich, in their innocence, had offered to store my trunk. Perhaps the ease that artists and the rich have in common is a thing simpler than those who see them veering toward each other recognize—a kind of childish directness and recognition which comes from a mixture of isolation and security. They have another, darker thing. Unconsciously, they wear their protections outside themselves like mollusks—artists, their admirers, those appreciative, palliating "acolytes," the rich, their servants. Had I told my hostess, we would have stormed the butler and dragged out the trunk ourselves, but she was in the country, and I, for that leave, had only my five pounds to get through London for two weeks, so the first day I stayed in uniform.

In that disguise, instead of the disguises in my trunk, London was open and free as air, with the troops on leave and the Americans pouring in and out of the huge Red Cross canteen near Leicester Square, where I could not go because I was in an Allied uniform.

I had tried it once, literally on orders from my commanding officer, who had met me on the parade ground at Turnbull St. Justin and had told me about having dinner in Bath with the head of the Red Cross canteen there. I could see the picture, all the officers in their splendor and the lady gracious in the evening. My CO had told her all about the American on the station and he said that she had said, "Tell her to come in and see us." This touched a loneliness for American voices I didn't know I had. On my next pass, I almost ran to the Red Cross, through the steady flow of GI's.

I was stopped at the desk and told that the canteen was not for Allied troops, while the passing GI's stared. I asked for the lady. She came roaring down the crowded hall, oh busier, busier than the lady at dinner with my CO. I explained who I was and thanked her for the message. She had, I suppose, forgotten it. She whipped out, in that edged voice Southern ladies reserve for the back rooms of their lives—not for gentlemen at dinner—that if I wanted to come to the canteen, I could put on a Red Cross uniform and work. Otherwise, the place was not for Allied other ranks to "hang out." I thanked her, stuck in the hallway among the GI's, some of whom had stopped to listen. For once in my life, I got the words there, instead of—impotently—later, as an *esprit d'escalier*. I said, "All right, and if you want to join the war sometime, I'll lend you my uniform," and left with my face burning.

So in London I avoided the Red Cross, knowing that inside there would be the girls I had grown up with, with their two kinds of voices.

And the British talked. They talked all that day—in the buses, in the pubs, in the queue for the concert at the National Gallery; they exposed their lives, their opinions. I have wondered since at this. For about five years after the war they ran down, no longer looked at each other in the street, entrenched themselves behind their newspapers, their pints, their doors. But during the war, they were, for once, the most direct people I had ever seen. Perhaps, being such a phlegmatic people, they needed the edging, the slow nightmare reality, to draw them out. The English were discovering each other with the freedom of strangers, lurched by war out of their silences, often friendly, sometimes with the direct belligerence of the stripped down.

In the late afternoon I remembered someone who might help me get to my clothes, a cousin of the people who were keeping my trunk, with whom I had had dinner before joining up in the reserved order of Quaglino's restaurant. I knocked on another of those thick, safe Mayfair doors. Down the block one of its twin houses had been hit. It looked like torn paper.

When he saw me he said, "For God's sake come in and have a bath. You smell like the people."

I realized why Mrs. Mead had been so silent at tea. It was the politeness of shock. I had been too shy to ask her for the rare hot water.

Later in the evening I rode back to Kensington, like Viv, in a taxi, with civilian clothes in a suitcase, ready to join the comfortable, muted roar of West End London.

Terence, Mrs. Mead and I sat balancing little trays for our supper. Now, seeing me in my own clothes, she began to talk. We had had tiny glasses of sherry while Mrs. Mead explained, throwing it off as an aside, that she had searched London for sherry because her physician ("He's the Queen's physician," she said) had advised her to have a little sherry before dinner. Every night afterward, when I had dinner there, she said the same thing, in the same offhand way, her thimble glass of sherry poised, her little finger straight.

That night Mrs. Mead was off duty. She explained that since the raids were "on" again she had arranged with the other tenants that Terence and I, who were on the top floor of the building, should sleep in the half basement. She said that Terence had carried our cots down in the afternoon. She apologized for not joining us by saying that she preferred staying "with her things," glancing around for safety at the finely polished furniture from Ireland. She took a sip of sherry and coughed the required dry little cough.

"After all, this sort of thing is new to you," she said. "I remember Dublin during the troubles. We sat on the veranda and watched the fires ten miles away."

Mrs. Mead was clinging to her furniture, her sherry and her manners, for safety. It was all she had against the alien blackness, the waiting, gray boredom and terror, confined in the floating room above the city.

Later in the night in dressing gowns and pajamas, Terence leading the way, we slipped single file down the six flights of stairs to the basement. One of the tenants stood at his door and tried to tease Terence as he watched the little procession of two, Terence carrying a muffled blackout candle high in front of us.

"Why are you bothering?" he called out.

"We are the wise virgins," Terence told him, and we marched on down the stairs, Terence with quiet dignity, I slinking along behind.

Two cots had been carefully made up at opposite sides of the large basement room. In the corner a huge pile of coke lay, ready for the boiler. Terence had made a little nest for himself; a chair with books on it stood beside his cot.

From my bed I could just see him across the room, propped up on pillows with that incredibly clean pajamaed look of a fifteen-year-old, reading one of the small Chatto and Windus editions of Proust by the dull light of the candle under its black shade.

During the days and in the evenings, I saw the war-lovers, not the few trigger-happy psychopaths beloved of the journalists, but the journalists themselves, the new generals with their red tabs, the aides, the tired ladies who kept the wartime salons in furnished apartments or half-empty houses. In the forties in London, it seemed to be the reign of women in their forties, amusing and attentive, with long fingernails, sleepless looking, spring-coiled. There was always an American officer or two, drinking in the atmosphere and the names, egg-breakingly careful of their new English manners, boned up on the nuances of Debrett. It was the most elegant cigarette exchange in the world.

They filled the Savoy, the Ritz, Claridge's. Tables were as hard to get as if London were in some carnival, and no one could remember the reason. Conversations come back as party fragments, voices of people lost in a new situation, clinging to old troubles and old standards, jostled at the same time by the new people and their war: a Guards officer, eighteen, pink and stupid, soon to be killed, sitting on the stairs of a house near Grosvenor Square, watching the dancers and saying, "Most of these people wouldn't have been here before the war. I wish you'd seen it then . . ." and over my shoulder in one of those mushroom clubs that sprang up overnight, "We're not in Debrett's, but we are in the back of Burke's."

"I know he's a good poet, but is he smart?" The literary and the snobs, the new officers, the tired, chic women, the cliques of pretty boys—all seemed to cling then to their groups as carefully as Mrs. Mead grasped at her sherry glass, intensifying their little certainties.

Late in the evening, walking through the blacked-out streets, hearing the haunting cries of "taxi!" from voices in all the accents of English spoken in the world, or stepping over the arms of sleeping children in the subway stations, flung out trustingly across the two-foot-wide path to the trains between the sleeping people, I would go back to Kensington and crawl in the window of the half basement to my cot. Terence, "waiting up for me," reading his Proust, would close his book and blow out the blackout candle so that I could undress in the dark and he could question me about where I had gone.

At about three o'clock in the morning the sound of it whistling toward us through the night woke us both, and we waited until time became space and waiting was all animal poise without thought for it to land. When it crashed, the street lit up outside like a lighning flash. Our windows imploded and tinkled down with a silly little noise. We huddled in our corners in the returned darkness.

Terence said, "Are you all right?"

I said, "Yes."

There was a long silence.

Terence said, "The next time this sort of thing happens"—and I waited until he went on from his corner of darkness—"I mustn't run over to you . . . and you mustn't run over to me———"

Outside in the street we could hear people running.

Somewhere in the square a few houses away the bomb had landed on a small hotel.

"——because if we were killed that way, mother would never understand."

All the rest of the night, in and out of sleep, I could sense the people turning in their beds, exposed and silent.

At the weekend I went to the country, this time leaving Paddington not with the lost girls but suitably suited and packed with care, to be met by car and taken to one of England's great piles of masonry—assembled without much imagination in the mid-nineteenth century from its ancient structure, still spoken of as being three hundred years old. A prewar Daimler picked me up at the station.

When the car rolled around the driveway to the house, making that soft crunch of expensive cars on well-rolled gravel, the maid stood at the door to show me to my room, in that ceremony of arrival which to an American seems like arriving at a country hotel where there are no other guests. I was shown through one of those barnlike stone halls. A fire burned in a replica of a medieval stone fireplace at the other end. I could just see a small brown woman sitting dwarfed in a tall-backed, heavily carved chair, alone. She did not look around. I was told that tea would be served in the drawingroom at four-thirty. It was then four o'clock, one of those vacant times of a winter afternoon.

Out of the windows of the high-ceilinged bedroom with the kind of furniture whose replicas used to be found in heavy apartments on Riverside Drive, I watched the half-mile-long sweep of the winter-dead formal garden, which rolled down to the Thames in the far distance. The box borders, in their careful patterns, looked as if they had been shaped so long ago by so many gardeners who had tended them into shape with care but without caring that they were no longer capable of shooting out new green in the spring, but would remain forever disciplined and trimmed. Through the trees of the private forest as tended as the garden, I saw a huddle of incongruous clean huts. Nobody moved in that architectural landscape which looked like a formal still etching of an eighteenth-century public garden, where there was no provision for humans, only for the carving of space and distance in a geometric design.

I was twenty-one years old and I felt lost and gauche and afraid to go downstairs. It may be four o'clock in the morning in hell, but in English country houses it is four o'clock in the afternoon, the morning a preparation for it, the evening a relief from it.

The brown woman was no longer in the great hall. Behind the carved door of the drawing room I heard a murmur, like whispering in a box. I pushed open the door. No matter where it is—in the kitchen of a cottage or, as the house party was, camped out around the tea table near the fire at the end of the enormous echoing drawing room—tea is cozy in England. I walked as if I were walking in an acre of plowed fields toward it. There were ten people, unsorted, withdrawn, around the tea table on the two large sofas. My hostess was serving. I went up and introduced myself, thanked her for asking me and waited to be introduced. This was too much to hope for. The English do not introduce. They simply, as my hostess did, hand you whatever drink is appropriate for the time of day, as if you had come in from the cold and needed it after an arduous journey, leaving you hanging on to it for safety and wait for you to move. I sat down beside the brown woman. Her hair was brown and drawn back. She wore brown tweeds, heavy brown brogues and wool stockings. I was able, by being almost entirely ignored, to watch and listen while the conversation grew again. The slight jarring wave I had made by entering the group was soon smoothed over. One of the dogs crept up and lay at my feet. I retired into the corner of the sofa, scratched the dog's ears and listened. Across from me an American major balanced his teacup, missing nothing, not saying a word. At the tea table with the hostess, an American war correspondent was taking in, by a sort of expansion into awareness of its importance, a conversation between a Conservative MP, the eighteen-year-old Guards officer I had met in London, the brown woman and the hostess. It was one of those easy, incestuous exchanges where Mountbatten is called Louis and a general with the deaths or lives of a million men at the tip of his pencil is called Bubby, or some such name. There had been a debate in the House of Commons, the kind of session they referred to as a "three-line whip," which meant, I gathered, that the lame, the halt and the blind were called in from their safe seats all over England and forced to sit up all night in order to stagger out for the division when everybody finally stopped debating. I stopped scratching the dog's ears. They were talking about the debate on the Beveridge Plan.

I drifted, for a minute, away from the warm fire and the lulling voices. One of Beveridge's aides on the plan had come to St. Justin-over-Water and had lectured to the troops on one of the most revolutionary and far-reaching economic designs for the future welfare of England ever, I suppose, devised by a group of responsible economic designers. On my way across the parade ground to the lecture, one of the WAAF Admin officers had stopped me and asked me to make notes on the lecture to report to the compulsory weekly discussion group, provided in King's Regulations for keeping WAAF in touch with the world. The hall, where usually we had two-year-old American movies about war, with P-40's painted to look like Luftwaffe planes, was about half full—it was not a compulsory lecture. There was not a WAAF officer in the room. I could pick out the usual faces—an ex-newspaper reporter, a Communist medical orderly, a lay preacher, my conchie friend, a few RAF officers, the station librarian. On the stage a tall man counted heads, then poured out to the gaggle of troops in the middle of the blank hall an impassioned plea for interest in the report. Much of the language I couldn't understand, but I caught the drift. Here, at last, was a concrete hope, instead of the vague promise of reward to the people couched in such subtle terms that it often seemed solid.

At the WAAF discussion group a few days later, I got up, shifted my notes through my fingers, looked at the girls, some of whom were looking out of the dirty window, some knitting, their eyes dull, waiting for it all to be over. I set the notes down on the table behind me and asked a question. "Why am I, the only foreigner on the station, telling you about the Beveridge Plan? Don't you care?"

One girl looked up from her knitting. "Because it's nothing but talk. They don't care," she said and went back to turning the heel of an Air-Force-blue sock. There, in the room, was all the inertia, the protective cynicism, of the ordinary people of England, represented by MP's who hardly knew their language, who "joshed" them with that arrogant jollity of British politicians campaigning on street corners, condescending to the pubs.

It was too great a calm to cut through—I went on with my notes, fast, to get it over. We were all relieved when it was finished.

My hostess was praising Quintin Hogg, the leader of the young Tories. "It's a shame he'll inherit," she said. Her voice, always, was vague, tired, withdrawn. She made her remarks as if they were her social duty and she wished we'd all go away. I wondered what it was that Quintin Hogg would inherit that was such a shame. The American correspondent, his mind grabbing bird-like at what they were saying, making the desultory conversation momentous for himself, asked.

"He'll be Hailsham." She was patient with him. "Of course he'll have to go into the Lords."

"Can't something be done about that?" he asked.

"Done?" The word dropped among the teacups. She had given him one of those one-word congés that women like her are trained for all their lives.

"But he said, 'If you do not give the people social reform, they will give you social revolution!' The House cheered him." That was me, my first words at tea. I didn't know about the silencing of obstreperous guests. There was a little drift of laughter around the room.

The old man at the fireside leaned back and informed. "My dear girl," he told me and all the rest, who, except for the correspondent were already sharing the joke, "don't you know that we always cheer when a member uses two political clichés in the same sentence?"

I wished then that I had a sock to retire to and knit.

The brown woman beside me decided that since I had a tongue, she would draw me out. She had a whispy, exhausted voice.

"I gather you've joined the Air Force," she said, also changing the subject. They were all tired of the Beveridge Plan. "You know, I think it's marvelous what the middle class is doing in the Air Force."

I looked so surprised that the old man began to inform again. "It is the Junior Service, don't you see?"

I didn't see anything but those mild, cool faces and his Blimp mustaches, that I couldn't believe were still worn by anybody in England. They were marvelous—as marvelous as the middle class in the Air Force. They were white, and they hung down on both sides of his healthy pink mouth and drooped below his chin. I suddenly realized that he was sweet looking, healthy and old and childish and innocent, and I wondered at the postwar political choice the British would have, except for a few rare men, after all the suffering, the work, the heartbreak, between such blind, comic, secure boobs and the bright groups of social paranoids in the Labour party, whom Laski called, with that condescension of the intellectual laborite toward his hard-bitten trade-union colleagues, "workers with the brain."

As we walked out of the drawing room at some command spoken so long ago that it was in the British genetic behavior, that we should entertain ourselves until we changed for dinner, the old MP strode beside me. I knew the stride. It was genetic too. It went with the pink looks that in certain Englishmen change imperceptively from a long, long adolescence to a kind of pleasant, good-mannered senility without anyone having the least idea, or caring, that it has happened.

"I think you're splendid to have come over," he boomed at me. "Know exactly what you're going through. Had the same thing in Octu in the last war."

In the gathering darkness, the American correspondent and I wandered through the formal garden that had a sense of having been deserted for a hundred years.

"God, these people are subtle. Talk about perfidious Albion. That was for my benefit," he was grumbling.

I didn't want to tell him that they hardly knew either of us were there.

"It's places like this that policy is made. Did you know there were two lords and three MP's in that room? They were *telling* me something."

I wanted to say, "But one of the lords was only a little pink peer." It seemed flippant. His solemn anger and my threatening flippancy were too small for the garden—or it was too spacious for humans, so we walked in it, not through it, treading the rolled lawn.

"Beveridge," he was still grumbling. "This country is going Communist after the war. They'll have a revolution." I thought of Viv and Sergeant Nightingale and Sergeant Smerd. I couldn't see them marching on the Savoy. There was no use trying to tell him. He already knew whatever he had decided to know and it had the insanity of thinking one understands a foreign language, having lost the key word.

"I sent my editor a cable," he went on. "He told me to find out if private enterprise is dead in England. It took me a week. I told him that there were only two places in England it was even mentioned—on a soapbox in Hyde Park and a few nuts in the agony column of the London *Times*."

T.S. Eliot once said that it was so hard to get a letter published in the *Times* letter column that he had a whole scrapbook of rejected letters. It is one of the most subtle barometers of informed English opinion. We walked on in the garden, the correspondent hot on the scent of intrigue in the drawing room by the perifidious lords and ladies—more legend to be added by his provincial mind to that of imperial intrigue among the teacups and over the port—while unrecognized, the true bent of England was being probed and gauged to prepare for the peace.

We turned back toward the high dark cliff of the house to change for dinner. Away in the distance I heard the laughter of children whispering across the great lawn.

In the candlelit dining room, I talked to my left and talked to my right and listened, my ears trained to listen through jamming to pinpoint the small voices on the R/T set, to conversations around the table. They seemed to have been picked up from old talk that had never had a beginning and would have no end. The correspondent (we were placed far apart, both being American, as if we had been husband and wife) was busy picking up and sorting out nuances. The American major sat with that look of awe that made me want to slap sense into my countrymen for being taken in by such small corners of England.

I heard my hostess say, "Dicky's like Alice in Wonderland in the House of Commons," and the little pink peer smiled through the candlelight, understanding.

I thought it was boredom that made her sit, retreating, a little from us all at the edge of the table, not even wishing any longer that we would go away. It was dinnertime, and decision of any kind receded back in the shadows beyond the candlelight, where the maids stood waiting to serve us. I heard her complain, lightly, once, as a hand came down to take her plate, that the war had taken all the men servants and that it was a nuisance to have to use sixty-year-old women in the dining room. I realized then that problems of war were pinpricks. What her cold face showed was not fear, but patience. She was simply waiting, using no energy in the wait, nor any charm, for things to be the way they were, and for the war, or life or whatever it was impinging on her ease, to be over. It was the "pure, colorless patience" of Rilke.

I heard her speak to me and flicked my eyes away from her face, ashamed of being caught staring.

"You were walking in the garden. As an American, you might be interested to know that it was laid out three hundred years ago. I'll show you the gallery after dinner." It was nearly time, as it had always been, to show the stranger the portraits.

"I heard children somewhere."

"Oh, yes," she said vaguely, "there are fifty of them evacuated here. They're in another part of the house. We don't see them."

"Who are they?"

"I have no idea." Whether she had or not, or whether on certain days she walked out to listen to that faraway buzz of life in the house, was none of my business.

After the ladies had had coffee, she took me along the cold gallery, warming toward me slightly as if, as a good hostess, she could replace the lack of heat. She walked along leaving a trail of vague regret that wartime was bad for the paintings, that the young were missing their ordered due—no debutante parties, no season, no gaiety. These things were to her as the thicker towels before the war had been to Mrs. Mead, and the mention of them gave the same brush of tragic wonder to her fine, stupid face. It was not her fault that I, at twenty-one, had already had my feet deeper in the mud of her country than she would ever have, but I saw no subtlety in the fineness of her breeding as she moved slowly down the gallery, her shoulders a little hunched under a shawl, complaining. I did see pathos, which even in the deaths of the young was as near to tragedy as she was equipped to draw. She had had the capacity to suffer bred out, buffed off—all that was left was an annoyance, an *agacement,* in its place.

Back in London, Mrs. Mead warmed her hands around her teacup and begged me with questions to give her the vicarious pleasure of being in the great house. When I told her about the interminable paper game played after dinner, trying my best to make a story of it, she said, "Oh yes, that's what they do," as if it made the world secure for a minute, as we put a charismatic force into the dull bodies of our gods, so that, intensified by all the sacrifices, it can be reflected back to us.

Other leaves come back not as events but as stops in time. One, a long-saved-for weekend at Claridge's, was so carefully planned that I hitchhiked in from the west country for it—toward an oasis of cleanliness and comfort, a reviving.

I stood on the side of the Great West Road, deserted in wartime, until a huge tanker truck stopped. I climbed up the ladder into a cabin soaked with the smell of gasoline and was driven toward London, sailing along high above the road, by one of the dirtiest, friendliest truck drivers that I found in all of my wartime hitchhiking. He was one of those pub philosophers so loved by the romantics who are supposed to be imbued with a simplicity of truth that all training and study cannot attain.

"It's like this, mate," he began each opinion, taking his hands off the large flat steering wheel of the three-ton truck as it bowled along down the empty highway. "You know, when Churchill said we will fight on the beaches, we will never surrender, I said to me old woman—this is it." The leader's words in that magic warring voice to the frightened people huddled around their little radios had pumped such warnings and such courage into the silent kitchens and the stilled pubs giving them, as it had given that man, licking his dirty hands, and holding forth, the illusion that they were making their own decisions.

As we neared London, still roaring through the suburbs, he said, "Look 'ere, mate. You're lucky. You're in a petrol lorry. I'll take you anywhere in London you want to go."

I said I would be grateful if he would put me off at Marble Arch.

He wouldn't hear of it. He said that we were mates and he was going to set me down right at my door.

I said I had someone to meet at Marble Arch.

"Naow come on, mate, don't be shy," he told me. "You couldn't 'ave even known wot time you were getting in Lunon. You're not getting out until you tell me where you're going. I can't let a nice foreign girl like you loose in Lunon."

It was fifteen feet down the ladder to get out. There was nothing else to do. We were, at that point, in full control of the middle of the Edgeware Road.

"I'm going to Claridge's," I said meekly.

Without another word, he swung down Oxford Street, out Bond Street, up Davies Street, and stopped the truck in front of Claridge's entrance.

The uniformed doorman reached up, opened the door, bowed very low and boomed, "Good evening, Madame," and reached up to help me down.

The driver drove off without saying good-bye.

I walked into Claridge's, filling the quiet foyer with gasoline fumes.

Cambridge comes back as it was during one of those idyllic spring weeks that make the English turn their heads toward the sun and relax their bodies and that allow them to be drenched with a scent and sweetness too rare not to be worshiped. Cambridge, emptied of its young men, except for those who wandered back nostalgically, on leave, had then a piercing sweetness about it—a light remembered from the Georgian poets of deaths felt more urgently, more loverlike—as people who are not and have never been at war, but who draw their experience from poets, expect it to be. Where there had been three hundred, there now were three pretty girls punting on the Cam and the laburnum was in bloom—the kind of elegiac scene in St. Mary's churchyard, mourning dead red lips, that had been written about by a generation more innocent and less self-conscious than ours. In and out of colleges, the boys on leave paused at doors of rooms now empty during the spring vacation and marked off their dead from their own memory.

In the evenings, the poets and the philosophers, working as conscientious objectors in the Cambridgeshire fields, gathered in the pubs. Muscular from their work, sad from alienation to the war, they talked in that split time of the past or of the future. Protectively courageous in their decision to have no part of it, they talked too about the war, obsessively, pent up by their self-imposed taboos.

Once, in a public comfort station below the square in Cambridge, a crazed old woman backed me into a corner and stuck her small gnarled face into mine, spraying malice and spit on me.

"It's the fault of women like you it's all happened. Dressed like that, sleeping with men. You ought to be 'ome 'aving babies. It wouldn't 'ave 'appened if the women were 'ome 'aving babies." She sobbed tears and spit at her trapped enemy until someone else came down the steps and she let me go free.

Chapter 7

There were still a few roses in the garden of the country house where WAAF were billeted when, two weeks before Christmas, the winter cold came. We wore our gloves in the little barracks set up in the once stately bedrooms. Girls sitting on their cots made mists of air as they talked, and piled their greatcoats over them as they, and I, went to bed in our stockings and sweaters, leaving only our noses out in the biting night air. On Saturday night I drew duty at the billet. I sat huddled under my greatcoat in the vast, cold, paneled drawing room, signing in WAAF as they came in for the night. Most of them had gone to bed. It was too cold to sit up. Far away, I could hear a cat crying. At ten o'clock, I heard the stamp of feet on the terrace, a murmuring of voices beyond the blackout curtains. A carol faltered, died, caught and rose outside. A small group of officers had gathered on the icy terrace, singing; fifteenth-century carols as light as the icy air drifted in the windows to us. The officers tramped away, laughing, warm with rum. I could hear them receding down the village street, leaving a deeper, emptier silence behind them.

But their coming had made the billet WAAF wander down in twos and threes for company in the empty great hall. They sat on the floor with their greatcoats over their shoulders and blew life into a tiny illegal fire of faggots in the huge blank Jacobean fireplace, leaving the room dark so that the fire would seem bigger and warmer. We were stripped down after the carols, remembering homes, separated from each other as we sought for a warmth that in that cold time was a warmth beyond the little fire and the presence of each other, an old warmth sought at that time throughout the Christian world, always sought but never quite found, that gives an undertow of sadness to a holiday where no sadness is recognized.

I looked over my shoulder into the near dark of the window seat. A girl I did not know sat very still, making not even the sound of breath, her face glistening with tears. I went over and sat beside her. She whispered to me, the words running easy like her tears, that her London home had been bombed, that they'd had ever such a lovely place. Her father had made most of the furniture himself and had raised a smashing garden, and her mum had made Christmas so nice for the children with a proper tree and all. Now it was all gone, all gone in one night—nothing left. After the story, she still made no sound of sobbing. She simply went on, looking into the winking fire, letting the tears run down without wiping them away.

One of the girls near us, leaning against the wall with her feet straight out toward the fire, had been listening to her story.

"Wa' a lie, Edwards." She looked up and grinned. "Don't let her 'ave you on. She's from Manchester. Never saw Lunon in her bloody life."

Some way it made her Christmas story more valid. I

thought she was crying for the destruction of dreams, and she had to make a dream that mattered.

Across the room I saw a new WAAF standing in front of the deal table, waiting to report to the "duty officer." The solid shoulders, the short hair, the ugly nice face, looked familiar.

I stepped over and around the bodies, all directional, mounds of greatcoats, their faces lit by the glow from the fireplace. The new WAAF's face was still in the shadow, half turned away.

"Viv?" I said to her back.

She turned around. "Wotcher, luv." She grinned. A year had changed her almost beyond recognition. The TNT dyed hair had grown out and was now dark in the firelight. She wore it in the regulation truck driver's pompadour. Her makeup no longer looked doll-like. She had a cavalier carelessness about herself in her WAAF battle dress, with her collar flipped like a fighter pilot. She exuded ease and belonging.

There was an empty cot in my room. Together we moved Viv's gear up through the darkness. She still had the shy voice, too gentle for her toughness. She looked at me and judged me coolly from way inside a life she had found and which agreed with her reality and what she knew of life; I had a sense of being outside it, outside a kind of adulthood that has to come early to be known.

"You stuck it this long," she said, after she had read my face. She went on putting away her gear. Down below us what had seemed so silent was a steady murmuring of the women around the fire, which drifted up the stairs.

"They took us off barrage balloons. I'm bloody cheesed off." The new language, for her, came as easy as breathing. "It was smashing. Now I'm a driver."

We went back down to the hall when she had finished, I back on duty, she to sit easily among the others around the fire. Someone had found a broken chair. It stuck up like burning bones, making a flaming arc of wood shooting out light.

Gradually the WAAF began to drift up the stairs to their rooms. Viv stayed beside the almost dead fire, not talking, just keeping me company until eleven o'clock, when I could go to bed. We were nearly whispering, because the silence of the billet pressed down on us from the space of the hall and the upper rooms, which seemed so empty and yet were so full of sleeping women, their wartime presence making so little impression on the house.

There was a shuffling, a sound of voices, an urgency, coming from the room on the upper landing. I heard someone run through the hall and start down the steps. The word "duty" is a demanding one. Like a mother, I was already alerted to trouble when the WAAF ran down the stairs and called out.

"Come quick. Come up here. It's the cats. The cats are in our room."

I was already running toward her when I realized that the whole thing was one of those mirages of panic that cats, mice and small strange sounds in the night could cause to flare up and then die down at once among the women.

"Well, get it out." I started to laugh.

"Please, miss, it's the cats. They're eating something in the cupboard." Not what she said, but the white glistening of her forehead in the last of the firelight made me realize that she was trying to keep from vomiting.

I ran up the stairs.

The WAAF were huddled at the door, waiting for me, for anyone with the name of authority.

Someone had slammed the cupboard door. I could hear the movement of the cats inside. The crying girl who had told the Christmas story was lying across her bed, her head hidden in her arms, her shoulders heaving.

When I opened the door the cats streamed out, jumping down around me from the top shelf, which had been meant to hold a lady's country hats on carved stands.

The box, partly wrapped in an old, sleazy candy-pink

nightgown, had been pushed to the back of the shelf, but the cats had pushed part of the nightgown away and had uncovered a blood-soaked corner.

There is a time of coolness in crisis when one lives within knowledge, moving through it until the need to act is over, suspending reaction for a time until action is complete. I got the box down from the cupboard and carried it past the sickened girls at the door and down the stairs and out into the night. At the second of recognition, without daring to look again, I knew that it had been a four- or five-month foetus and the dead remains of its placenta.

The ground was not yet too hard to dig. Viv and I dug a hole in the garden under the roses and buried it. By the time we had finished, the reaction was making me shake with recognition. We went back up into the room where the crying girl was still lying on her cot under the naked light, isolated from the others, who had drawn away from her as from death. I sat down on the cot beside her and felt her head. It was cold.

"How long ago did this happen?"

"A week," her voice was muffled by her own tears. The others, across the room, were straining to hear.

"Have you reported to the MO?" I asked her.

"I can't do that. I'm married. My chap is stationed in Africa. We've not seen each other for a year. 'E's my chap."

"I'll go with you into town tomorrow. We'll go to a civilian doctor."

"How did you do it?" Viv asked, practically, from the other side of the cot.

"Knitting needle."

Viv looked at me above the girl's head. "We never had to worry on barrage balloons," she said. "You try heaving them cables. It was a proper joke. Why didn't you get rid of it?"

"I kept waiting until I could get to water. The pond's froze over, and the river . . . You won't report it?" The girl had opened her eyes and was trying to read my face.

"Of course not."

We lived in the underworld and had our survival rules, and to tell those faraway people, the officers singing on the terrace, was unthinkable.

"Get out of it, you filthy thing," one of the girls screamed and kicked at something in the doorway. A cat howled and ran away down the stairs.

When the lights were finally out and I lay taut with cold and the kind of physical despair that the piecing together another human's secret terror can bring, I listened to the quietness of the other wide-awake women around me in the room.

The next afternoon Viv scrounged a truck to drive us in to the village GP. He took a long time to answer the office bell. He led the Manchester WAAF roughly by the arm into his office. They were gone a long time. When they came back, she had been crying again and the GP looked exhausted. All I remember about him are a more-than-physical fatigue and an old brown jacket with a button hanging loose.

He said, "I ought to report this."

No one answered.

"She's all right." He looked at her. "I'm taking a chance, you know. You girls . . . I won't report it if you promise to come back in three days. She's all right," he added to himself as he went back through the office, and we heard the door to the living part of his house open into more silence, then close again, leaving us there with the old copies of *Punch*.

As we drove back through the village, we saw a few little trees trimmed by the children with the thin aluminum strips they had picked up from the ground— dropped by German planes. Someone said that they were to confuse our radar. I don't know. They made pretty icicles inside the windows at dusk, before time to pull the blackout curtains.

All the attempts to know each other, to live together, seemed to have been stripped away by memories. We were all someplace else. Viv swerved to avoid a cyclist and muttered, "Fuck."

By Christmas Eve, the fog had frozen to the trees and the stubble in the fields, making pale halos over everything. There was no flying. Out beyond the great window of the flying control room, the grayish whiteness spread as far as we could see over the great flat space of the airfield. Those who had not drawn a Christmas pass sat, frozen away from each other, waiting in their boredom for the holiday going on somewhere else to be over, watching the post more carefully for the small brown wartime parcels, secretly as hopeful as children.

In the evening we drifted, as the others did, down to the tiny village pub. The publican had lit a fire, and we cringed close to it, drinking beer and, finally as we began to thaw out, singing together. At first we tentatively sang carols, and then, strongly, the songs we knew together, the Air Force songs, safe and raucous, all sung that night as quietly as if they were carols.

"They say that this Air Force is a mighty fine place, but the way that they treat you is a bloody disgrace," quietly the tune of "The Mountains of Mourne" filtered through the pub.

At breakfast on Christmas Day, there was a large notice that dinner would be served to all ranks not on duty at 1300 hours in the airmen's mess. Viv, with that pleased surprise she could call up, simply, for any promised "treat," was excited. "It'll be smashing," she said. I felt jaded by what was another of those tired attempts to recognize life on the station, and I wondered how tradition—or King's Regulations—dealt with the problem of Christmas.

The airmen's mess was hung with colored paper. The tables were set in long, long rows, with our places so close together that our shoulders touched. There was a tiny glass at each place, and from the kitchen whose floor I remembered so well came, for once, the smell of good food, of roast turkey, and the sweet scent of hot candied fruit. We sat and waited, saying little, listening to laughter from the kitchen.

The first officers came in, balancing plates, to serve

the other ranks, all flushed from drinks at their mess party, and the steam from the hot kitchen. The other ranks sat, reverent and silent, as if they were Christmas beggars, while those brash men and women, in their one-day-of-the-year roles as servants took on the jollity and gestures of the tradition of the British Forces, reverting for Christmas into Good King Wenceslas, serving the poor.

I had a sudden horror that tradition might have provided that they stagger about, trying to wash our feet.

Christmas is gesture, and if the impetus is gone, the gesture goes on. In the Forces there was no time and little place for the reason to thrust through the gesture. We were never more in the wrong place at the wrong time than sitting crowded together in the airmen's mess, saying little, eating our best dinner of the year, while over our humble heads the officers played. Once in a while I would hear one of the other ranks say, "Thank you, sir," as he or she cringed aside to give room to be served.

Viv was eating as if she had never eaten before, stopping to sip at her wine ration, nudging me from time to time to whisper, too awed by the atmosphere of ceremony to raise her voice, "Look at the Admin officer. She's 'ad one too many."

The Admin officer, rosy with the day and the easy playful attention of the men, was having a spendid time, booming out, "Now, girls, eat up. It's only once a year."

I didn't wait for the mince pie. The place was too closed, too heavy, too intrusive of the loneliness I needed to hold to me. I managed to get away from the close quarters of the table and out into the clean, cold air of the parade ground. I walked, huddled in my greatcoat, breathing mist into the frozen air, until my body was warm and the pull of memory was over and I could go back to the trappings of the billet and the women, back into the time again.

When I turned into the billet gate, it was dusk. The rooms were alive with sound, the fire had been lit again. Even the girl from Manchester sat, warm and belonging, with the others. From the good food and the ceremony and the cold, they had conjured up the stretched, full time of Christmas afternoon, as it has always been when the sad heart of it is obliterated by food and habit and it is over at last, and the day stretches toward evening.

I went through the great hall and up to my cot, my own center. On my bed lay a pack of cigarettes. Someone had left a present.

Viv followed me up. "I've brought your mince," she told me.

I sat with the dark gray mince pie in my lap and began, at last, to sob.

She watched me.

"In' it odd?" she asked. "You could take the other night, and you can't take this. I dunnow. Some people." Then she added, less irrelevantly than she thought, "They didn't mean no 'arm."

Chapter 8

What is the quality of war that so many miss and that makes peace seem dull, undirectional, lacking in zest? What is it that we, as a generation, have "told around" as if it were a secret we could not name? I think that it was the opposite reaction to that of the frightened, withdrawn, taut women. It was edge, a full awakening, an adrenal heightening caused by fatigue and an atavistic sense of danger that made the senses expand and extend, that made most of the young who could bear the extension of awareness miss forever that singing of the warning senses, that cat awareness. In peacetime, it has to be developed individually, not in the dangerous, shortcut imposition of circumstances war provides.

But for the already sensitized, that awareness can be developed beyond the physical capacity to carry it, as if a machine were overloaded. Those already suffering (in the Biblical sense of allowing) their worlds with their senses extended normally to their full capacity—the artists, the highly trained and evolved minds—went, unless they were blessed with extraordinary physical cushions for the shock, beyond their capacity for fatigue, for a neural bearing of what they saw and what they knew. The wave of deaths and suicides of highly intelligent men, the burning-out of promise, the lack of large, sustained bodies of works of art in the talented, after the war, were partly the result of this overloading, and in the rest who had been forced alive, there was a residue of sadness for what they could no longer achieve on their own. They tried to go back to peacetime, to sleep, but they had been as fully alive as wary animals, and they remembered it and wasted themselves in nostalgia.

In the already aware, it sometimes had a terrifying effect—nothing was closed—and we lived as seers, a little ashamed of what we saw. My hearing, as a result of listening through jamming on the set, became dangerously extended, uncensored. The other senses were affected too. Sight, for the flicks of danger, of life, was as a hunter's who perpetually walks the fields, alert for the movement of bird wing. The tactile nerves were exposed—the touch wary and delicate from the running of the machines; the memory of a mane rising along one's back in the primordial reactions to danger and the night, were a chill warning that would be left over long after the danger had passed to rise impotently, triggered by memory.

Then, in some of us, the awareness stepped over the line, went too far.

I knew it first on the day I was moved to the country house billet outside the station in the village of Combe Waring, a mile and a half across the flat fields from Turnbull St. Justin. My gear had been taken out to the billet, and when I came off the set at midnight, in the deep twilight of double summer time, it was a gentle warm summer night. The trees were at their fullest, the wheat fields across from the straight road that ran along one side of the station and past the large solid building of the permanent officer's mess were already showing white—drained of their day yellow by the coming night. It was one of those low-pitched, lulling nights where what small bird sounds I could hear drifted clear over the wide fields. Even on the station, through the iron webbing of the fence to my right as I cycled along, there was no one moving. The first stars were beginning to show. Not quite used to the time, I wondered why there was no night flying, then I remembered that it was Saturday, and midnight, and that the station personnel would be spread on leave, on weekend passes, on day passes, away from the airdrome. Ahead of me I heard the first whisper of music from the officer's mess. It stopped. Someone had opened, then closed a door. It was a comforting sound. I was tired, at ease, off-duty at last and pleased at being in a house after the pinched ugly quarters of the station.

That was at one minute—at the next I was enveloped in and blinded by terror.

I cycled in full panic down the empty road, trying to get through the terror. It clung to my back as I went down a steep little hill, where, at the bottom, the road turned sharply left where the old road had been lopped off by the airdrome, across a little bridge, up the hill opposite and a mile straight between the fields to Combe Waring. I did not stop until I had turned into the village street. I could hear voices, and I slowed down. In a few minutes, out of the exposed fields and under the trees of the village street, twilight had turned into night, and I knew I had left the terror behind me.

I sat on my cot, alone, the five other women not yet there. I could hear voices on the terrace outside the house. It had been too dark to see what the billet looked like, but I could tell by the room that before the war it had been one of those small manor houses deceptively close to a village street but which front onto a large garden, with the fields rolling out beyond in the distance. The room had been a bedroom. My cot was pushed near a pretty little disused fireplace. Across the room cupboards had been built into the wall. The woodwork was delicate; the broken mirror over what once had been a dressing table but now was empty except for a gasmask cover someone had left reflected only a little light from the hall and my white, sickened face.

I knew that unless I hunted down the panic, I could not go on, exposed to it at any time and in any place, ready to drench me with a primordial blinding terror. I tried to think back to where it had happened, and I forced myself to recall the riding, the fine night, the descent of the night fear. I was sure that it was a compound of fatigue and alertness from the set, triggered by some sound in the night. I remembered the door's opening and closing. It had happened after that, and it had not been triggered by sound, but visually—a not-seeing and a clinging, tactile sense. I saw again the vast shadows of two great old trees standing side by side between the fence and the road to my right—two old trees, nothing else, no flick of a moving shadow—just the stillness and the two trees and the panic.

The next morning the sun was out, and I had the whole morning to myself, off duty until four o'clock. Rations had been put into the old kitchen for the WAAF on shift. I made cocoa and sliced the gray bread on a scrubbed wooden table large enough to have once served a large household. In the quiet morning, I tried to see a memory of the house as it had been. The sun poured into the kitchen and made shadows of the dish racks across the wall above the big sink. The glass doors of the cupboards were dull, uncleaned. All the dishes and pans of the household had been removed. I could conjure up little of cooks and housemaids. The room was too big and too dead. I carried my cocoa and bread and marg out on to the long empty terrace which ran the length of the house. The grass of the lawn was uncut, the garden untended. All along the terrace, the high mullioned windows were opened and the breeze blew into a paneled central hall with a carved stairway at the end, which I had run up without noticing the night before. At the other end was a fine, intricately carved Jacobean fireplace. The room was quiet, empty except for a folding chair and table, where the "duty officer," usually an Admin corporal, sat at night to check in the WAAF.

I knew, in the quiet morning, that there had been no panic the night before, that it had been a warning of my own senses, revolting against long-sustained exposure and exploitation. Even sitting there on the stone balustrade of the terrace, with the four-story Jacobean house front rising behind me, safe and surviving, the perpetual enemy jamming buzzed in my head; it was constantly there; turned on as soon as I awoke, as it was with all of us who had been on the set more than a few months. I was a little afraid that the panic had been the first sign of what was called "signals shock." We talked about it during the nights on watch, alert to its signs. Girls who had it were taken off the sets—too inefficient to go on. The little Marconi transmitter-receivers were too far from the enemy to be knocked out, but the operators, with their frail, delicate human aural sense, were as near as the headphone to the ear. They could be reached by the incessant sound, repetitive as dripping water, more carefully designed to jam the neutral circuit.

By afternoon I had convinced myself that nothing outside myself had happened, and I rode back down the long straight road between the ripe fields, the day lonely, the larks, which do shoot up straight out of sight from the ground, trilling. I went down the long hill to the bridge, slowed and turned at right angles up toward the station gate, pushing the bicycle slowly, liking the day and wondering how, in the panic of the night before—which by then was hard to remember—I had managed the strength to turn the angle, cross the bridge and ride up the other hill in the dark.

The two old trees were up ahead now, to my left. They looked from the distance as safe and calm as the great trunks and gently moving branches always had been, as expected in their images as the larks.

This time I walked, as through a separation in space, into the clinging tactile terror.

I began to run down the sunny road past the trees, my eyes, in the eye of terror, tight shut. It receded behind me, but I was too panicked to get back on the bicycle. I just kept on running, pulling the bicycle along with me.

All through the eight hours on the set I knew I would have to pass the trees again, and I knew I could not do it alone. By this time, having passed twice through the eye of the terror, I could pinpoint the center of greatest intensity. It was the first of the two trees, which were so alike, yet so horribly unalike. It was all, at that point, I dared to examine. I knew I would have to have help until I either grew through the panic or found out, logically, what it was.

All they had in common was the tree. Without allowing themselves to know—or rather, except in flicks of awareness, to let me know they suspected—three friends without fail took turns walking me past the tree when I had to go by it at night, never, except once, putting any question into words. In that atmosphere of mixed ennui and edge, they simply turned up at midnight, taking turns without knowing each other, each with an empathy toward the fear, connected only by the situation and their own intuitive understanding.

The first was a leading aircraftsman in signals who, on his day off, rode his bicycle off to those villages which had tiny nonconformist chapels and preached as a lay preacher. He had a country, working-class mind, which in England turns into a kind of unchanneled, untrained Tolstoian vision, fusing left-wing thinking with a pantheistic deity, speaking in the concepts of natural poets. Once he made me stare at the sky until I had a sense of its stillness and of the turn of the earth underneath my body. His country gentleness had great passion in it, without fanaticism. But the center of his ambition—if the deep desire to tell the others about how incredibly beautiful he found the earth, as if he were in love with it, could be called ambition—was to speak once in Hyde Park. I hope he never achieved it. In the broken, stomped grass of the Park Corner, with the buses groaning by at Marble Arch and the city hecklers gnatlike in their sharp amusement, his voice, calling above the wide expanse of dead concrete, would have been too small.

As we neared the area of the tree at night, he would sense that my back was beginning to tense and would simply bury my head on his shoulder and walk me through the area of terror, seeming to know exactly where it began and ended, but completely unafraid. Whatever it was, it was of his beloved earth, and he had no questions for it. At the little bridge where the old road was cut off by the building of the airdrome, he would stop and shake hands for a formal, shy goodnight, and I would walk on up the hill through the lowering darkness, which never seemed to be black night, unafraid, until I came to the dark avenue of the village trees, and the safe quiet of the billet.

Once he showed me how the natural road had once run before its blotting out of the airdrome. It had been a country crossroad. Now its two sides were gone, bulldozed away, leaving only the sharp curve.

The second escort was a wing commander, a pilot— in peacetime an economist, or would have been, had he not joined the Cambridge Squadron at the beginning of the war and brought into it a sardonic civilian wit that had marked him as a rebel. He told about the squadron's being made to march down the street in Cambridge, uniformed in the hated student pilot's battle dress with white training flashes on their embarrassingly jaunty caps—on which each student had lettered HMS Humiliated. He talked about the beginning of the war—the amateur's war, the time of the civilian volunteers unmuted, as we were by 1943, by being in a huge ungainly conscript force—as if it were a far place and a long time past. I think he was right. Those bright young men were the last to taste the final demand of individual combat in that delicate meeting of the perfect machines, man and the Spitfire, gauged to the outside capacity of humans to function in complete accord with the mechanism and the elements. The balance would be broken, the machine made too fast for such close, sensuous maneuverability ever again—and those who survived were spread out, by 1943, through the training commands, too old, at twenty-three or twenty-four, too overused, to fly combat missions.

So in the summer nights when it was his turn, he would guide me past the area of the tree, pressing the back of my neck between his fingers to urge calm and guide me as we walked, me with eyes tight shut, through to the bridge. He teased and sometimes tried to question me, but he never pushed the questioning, sensing how much I could tell, and he never questioned the fear itself. He had respect for it. I think he had been in it sometime, but he never said. He only kept up the sardonic banter to keep my mind as much away from it as he could. He offered his empathy with strength and wit.

The third was the station librarian. A civilian unable to pass his physical examination for the Forces, he would walk through the station in one of those baggy sports jackets that are for English intellectuals, a badge of minority respectability never bought but always hung on the body, as the oatmeal cardigans of the women. They rise in an arc at the back, over the seat, and dip forward at the front, already shaped for too many books in the pockets. His face was thin, his head jutted out and threw itself forward as he walked, as if he were balancing an invisible knapsack on his back, in the prewar socialist, intellectual, liberal, sandals he wore summer and winter. When we walked together, he talked on and on, throwing out his long arms as if he were throwing ideas compounded of Jung, the nines of Plotinus, Gurdjief and the cabala out of his mouth and catching them in his hands. Through a mist of occult abstractions, he would walk toward the tree, and he would try to keep the fear beginning to flower across my back down by words—any words—within the protection of abstraction. He did not sustain me with his arm but with his words, and I would cling to them as if they were flesh.

Once he caught my arm, as we were entering the area of the tree.

He said, "Stop!"

I did, quivering.

"It's time you faced this," he said in his schoolmaster voice, trying concrete psychology because the abstractions had failed.

I stood, my eyes tight shut, afraid to move again.

"Look at it. Look at the tree."

He saw my eyes, shut against it.

"My God, you'd think a man had hanged himself in it."

I was gone, running, all the way to the billet a mile away, the run slowing to a staggering dream movement, like running in a dream.

I had to face, after that, that he had, somehow, broken through to the shadow of some fact, not about my own fear, but about the tree itself. In the day, off duty, sitting in the cozy, fuggy kitchen of the village postmistress, drinking tea, I began to ask questions.

She thought that it was funny, because if there was one thing that she knew about us, it was that all Americans came to England looking for ghosts. She said that she'd been there all of her life and had heard nothing. She told me about "before the war," before the airdrome, when she was a child. She and her brothers would take their picnic down to what had been the crossroads deep in the ripe fields and catch trout in the little stream and have their tea under the two trees, which made a great summer canopy of shade.

But any fact was better than not knowing. I think there is a quality of a question unanswered in the word "haunted." I was being haunted by the tree. It would not release me by giving forth its facts. By day, finally, I could walk by it without panic, but there was always left near it a sense of vacuum or of a confinement of my skin or of my ability to move easily that I could not or would not name.

Some time after Christmas, my watch mate and I were moved back onto the station, so that we could sleep in the daytime, off watch. She was a honey-blonde girl from Aberdeen, lovely looking, neat, quiet, as sensible as her always perfectly laundered shirts and polished shoes. It was balm to share the room with her. At night, when she came off duty, one of the student pilots would call for her, standing formally in the dark lower hall in one of those gentle habits that resurged from a world of peace and was set down in the strange environment of the station. They would stroll toward the WAAF quarters in the blackout as if he had waited to see her home from school. They were "walking out" as formally and conservatively as if her sea-captain father waited in some parlor in the north of Scotland for the precious feminine object to be handed from fiancé to father for safekeeping. She had the look and way of a woman who would be cared for that way all of her life.

But as we slept through the morning, I would wake to find her, asleep and dreaming, sitting upright in bed, manipulating the empty air in front of her, tuning the R/T set and calling out in panic, "Hello, Nemo. Hello, Nemo. Repeat, repeat," trying to bring in a nightmare plane. I would touch her shoulder and wait until she lay down again, muttering in a dream change, the frustrated tears covering her sleeping face.

The tree receded into dreams and nagging questions—but I had no need to go near it again. It began to combine in my nightmares with all the other images of fear. I could not quite let it go, having no answer. There was no more use to question. The station personnel were new, wartime people. The only person I knew in Combe Waring—the postmistress—still laughed about the Americans, giving me tea from time to time, enjoying the search.

In 1946, when I had been long away from the station, when the war was over and the requisitioned houses had been turned back to their owners, when the senses were calmed and slurred again, I went back once more to Combe Waring to question for the last time before I put the tree, along with the rest of the memories, away in my mind for all the years from then to now. In recall, the time between has disappeared, and I am again, as I was on a lovely peacetime day, riding back by the tree along the road to Combe Waring. The station was nearly deserted. The wartime camouflage of the buildings was flaking away; the dead-looking overgrown paths, the neglected growth, was now pushing through the asphalt of the station, while along the civilian road, the countryside seemed to have come alive again.

It was only a tree. I could go up and touch the rough bark. The haunting fear had been a revolt of my own senses. I rode on into Combe Waring to have tea with the postmistress for the last time.

The WAAF, the harsh-sounding trucks, the issue bicycles were gone from the village street. The gardens were cared for and heavy with roses; the churchyard was clipped and clean; some of the house doors were newly painted.

In the front garden of the postmistress' house, there were delphinium and lupines where there had been cabbages and terrible little hard Brussels sprouts on their awkward stalks. Sitting in the kitchen, she brought up the tree first. I had almost decided not to ask her anymore. The haunting was over. I had accepted—and time had begun to cure—what I knew was its cause, as people all over England were gradually thawing from the numbness of the war.

She told me that Mr. Nelson, the owner of the house I had been billeted in, had returned. He was a very old man, one of those amateurs of local history that exist in their gentle scholarship in every English county, the genealogists, the collectors of centuries of local gossip.

After I told her good-bye, I went past the Jacobean house and stood by the stone pillar of its gate. The roses were trimmed and the heavy door polished so that it shone nearly black in the late afternoon sun. Then I turned in and went up the walk, getting my story ready as I went.

Somewhere inside the house a bell clanged. No one came, and I was just turning away, relieved, when the door swung back, no longer making the neglected creak that I remembered. An old man stood watching me without a word, and I made my speech to him before I realized that he was a servant. I had expected age, and he was so old and seemed so in command. I told him that I had once been billeted in the house and that I had become interested in local county history. I asked if I could see Mr. Nelson.

"Mr. Nelson is very old," he said, as if I ought to know it, "but I'll see."

The door closed again, and I waited, suddenly excited without wanting to be.

They were right. Mr. Nelson was the oldest-looking man I had ever seen; his age had given him a kind of transparency of skin over his nose and his bony head. His hair was frail and silver, and he wore, I'm sure, the last velvet skullcap and library jacket of the antiquarian out of the whole genre of the conservative ghost-story literature of England. He seemed to have dressed proprly, as the English do, to tell me the end of my story.

I began, stumbling because his face was cold, to make my excuses.

He only questioned, "Yes?" as if I were trying to sell him something and he wished I would go away.

I said, "Do you know the two trees in front of the officer's mess on the right side of the road, coming toward . . ."

He reached out and took both my hands.

"My dear," he said, "can you divine water?"

I didn't know what he meant. He drew me into the now glossy, alive corridor. Through the door to the right I could see the Jacobean great hall and smell the compound of polish and cooking and flowers. Where the windows had been bare, there were heavy curtains. Those old men had managed in a short time to get rid of the smell of neglect and wartime dust and emptiness, to replace it with the smell of age and care that had been interrupted by the war. The house was, as it had been, fused with the life they wanted. We had been cleaned out and forgotten.

He drew me into the library. His books had been put back in the empty shelves, all the way to the ceiling. There was the correct smell of calf bindings and of leather chairs—secure and rich. When he shut the door, I began to feel again the fear I thought had been gone so long.

"I am going to show you something, since you already know," he said and pottered among his books looking for something. "Though it's most extraordinary that you should. Well, I cease to question. At my age, I cease to question, I'm nearly ninety, you know."

He motioned me over to the library table and laid out a local map. The date was 1750. Without a word he drew his finger across Combe Waring, down the road to the little bridge where the crossroads had been for centuries before the imposition of the airdrome. I saw the finger trace up the road to the right. There, on the site of the tree, was the public gallows.

"A friend of mine found this map and a journal years ago. We never told. The story had been forgotten, and we didn't want to frighten the children." His voice went on quietly in the safe room. "Two sailors had jumped ship and stolen some money. They got as far as Combe Waring and fell to quarreling over the spoils. One of them killed the other—it was said for only three guineas. He was tried and sentenced to be hanged in chains. It was the slowest form of hanging, to be put on the gibbet loaded with chains and have them gradually weight a man's life out. Sometimes it took several days . . . sometimes hours . . ."

It hadn't been a vacuum. It had been a sense of weight, of being trapped.

"The sailor took a long time to die. As he died, at first the people came to watch, but he cursed them and cursed the ground and they couldn't stand to watch anymore."

I knew that. I had passed into the horror of the crowd, still soaking the ground around the tree.

"It was the last hanging in chains in the west country. Even those people, so used to death, couldn't stand it anymore.

"Don't worry my dear," he said, "it won't happen often in your life. The circumstances have to be right and you have to be very tired. We were all so very tired. One is, in wartime. Do you know I've been through three wars now—and I fought in the Sudan and on the northwest frontier of India . . ." He patted my hand. "Don't ever go there. Now I'll ring for tea."

"Oh," he added as he pulled the bell cord. "I'd rather you didn't tell this. It might frighten the children."

The rich quietness of the library, the arid touch of his clean hands on the map as he put it away, the genteel acceptance of the Devil in a calm scholarly way were sucking out the air and light and blood from what I had known. I said in my mind silently to his secure old back, "In the cupboard of your morning-pretty bedroom, where you are brought tea and you read the *Times* and think about the nicer occult mysteries, I found the aborted baby, not yet formed, got at by the cats. It's buried in your garden. Can't you hear the girls move and cry? Oh, this is no subject for a library, and there was the sailor finally giving up and pouring out his mean manhood like glue to make a little legend."

I had forgotten that there are no surprises for old men, only a careful censorship of mind to make life bearable. He was handling the diary lovingly as he put it away, because it was old and of value.

So Mr. Nelson was not his name, and Combe Waring was not the village, and he must long since be dead. I have not broken my promise. I think he would understand that this was about war, a part of it. After all, he had seen so many.

Chapter 9

There were days of release, some by a sort of earthy, unnamed Tao, some by flight, some, as in the unbearable times of peace, by conversion.

The WAAF mess was separate from the airmen's in the cookhouse. At the top of the wide concrete stairway, at noon, I could see how full the mess was by the solid wall of WAAF caps, hung on hooks. I could never understand, in that wall of blue conformity, why we didn't get mixed up, but we never did. The caps had taken on the shapes of their owners. I could tell when the fitters and riggers were in the mess. They took pride in the oil spots, the faded blue from cleaning; they wore their peaks so bent that they curled snugly across the inevitable front pompadours. The Admin caps looked hardly worn, unkneaded to the individual head, the signals caps a little jauntier, their insignia almost without design, polished flat and shining in the long nights. We wore our caps like individual badges. I can still see my cap, from across the hall, always standing out to me from the others, so exactly alike, molded so differently.

From inside the mess, there was, until one-thirty, a roar of noise, gradually quieting with the time, the swill smell of the food—in winter, the smell of wool and grease and women shut in the room behind the windows fogged and dirty from the steam of the hot plates. Over it all, in the next room, the "recreation room," the radio was turned up full blast for Workers' Play Time, or the news. It was the BBC Light Program—never changed, just turned on and left on, blasting, until everyone had gone and some lost WAAF remembered to turn it off. No one listened to it except a very few officious ones, myself included, who still, like civilians, listened to the news.

One day, late for lunch, I raced up the stairs, flung

my cap on a hook among the others and ran into the recreation room just in time to hear the BBC voice saying, "That was the news . . ." The British had landed at Salerno a few days before, on European soil again for the first time since Dunkirk. There were rumors of Italy's surrender. Under the mainstream of the blast from the radio, a very small, baby-blond fitter lay curled up in a broken chair, her eyes closed, a long smudge of grease on her little face.

I touched her and asked, "What was the news?"

She looked at me, surprised. I realized that she had been asleep. "I don't know, luv, the war ain't over yet." She closed her eyes and turned in the chair. The roar of laughter from the crowd of factory workers from somewhere in the Midlands, being entertained by a comic, went on over her head.

That, or "Stow it, luv. Can't you see I'm asleep," would probably have been my answer at Salerno as well from troops off duty for a snatch of rest, doing their job, living their releases within it as best they could until it was over and they were free again. The language of battle, of sectors and vectors and movements was left for briefings, for newspapers or for the cool precise voice of the BBC. I remembered, later, a headline in a British newspaper. After years of the familiar voice beginning, "Here is the news read by Alvar Lidell," the headline read, "Here is the Square bashed by Alvar Lidell." In initial training, the hours of drill were called "square bashing." I wondered then if he ran to the radio, off duty, pushed the unconscious, the withdrawn, the patient attenders out of the way and listened, alone, to the news.

Gradually, I brought more of my belongings to the station, as the others did. The inspections were less rigid, so that small photographs of soldiers and airmen, in their jaunty caps, grinning—there seemed to be one pose—began to appear beside the cots; a knitted tea-cozy, purple and black, was left in the kitchen; civilian underwear, fancy tooth mugs, make-up—all the personal feminine litter—was strewn over the billet, to be shoved out of sight at any warning. As I judged by belongings so was I judged—by those and, as always, by habits.

"I'd like to make friends," the girl in the next cot said to me once, "but you brush your teeth twice a day—I'm not used to the likes of that. I only brush mine once, at night. I think that's enough." "Enoof," she said, north country.

I brought the few records I had and found a portable phonograph in the station library. There, off duty, I would find my own kind of relief alone, at peace, playing them in turn, forgetting that the sound of the records carried far out over the blank road below the opened window.

One evening I sat, gazing at nothing outside the window, listening to the light sad *Requiem* of Fauré, with its pure children's voices. Down below me, in the distance, I saw a lone WAAF, wandering, not walking fast enough to be going anywhere. It was the station eccentric, a red-haired girl whose relief from the untenable life was so complete within her that she had not refused but simply sloughed off any learning of a job that required other people. She moved gently within her safe world, Bartleby the Scrivener, preferring not to. No one knew anything about her. She told nothing, made no contact, kept just enough on the right side of the crime in King's Regulations called "dumb insolence" to be left alone. Finally, because no one knew what to do with her, she was given charge of shoe repair for the WAAF. All to herself in her one-room shoe shop, she accepted the worn shoes without a word, giving out tickets, returning patched shoes, her head turned away—the only contact was the exchange of tickets and shoes and, once in a while, by mistake, the touching of hands.

She stopped in the road and stood there, her head forward. I thought she had seen something in the road. The record ended and I turned away from the window to change it. When I went back to sit in the window she was gone.

There was a knock at the door and the red-haired girl put her head in.

"May I come and listen?" she said. "I love the Fauré *Requiem.*"

"Oh, yes," I began, but she withdrew from any more talk. She let herself down to the floor, lay her head back against the wall and closed her eyes, her face in complete repose as she listened to the sexless boys' voices.

When it was over, she began to talk. "You have the Brahm's violin concerto, too. Sometimes I come and listen from outside. I knew you wanted to be alone, but tonight, I couldn't bear hearing it from so far away."

She was quiet for a minute.

"Do you want to hear some more?" I asked her.

"No, I couldn't bear it all at once," her voice was beautiful, low pitched, cultured.

"Then come back."

"May I do that?" she got up to go. "You know, this whole thing is wrong—this life—terrible. I don't know what to do about it. I see you, going about the station, talking with anybody—I wonder how you do it when you know this." She motioned vaguely at the air where the music had been, including me in it, taking it for granted that if one world were accepted, there could be no other.

On the roads, in the mess, she would not speak to me or any of the others, but often, in the evening when she heard the music, she would come back to sit in the same position and listen. I had entered her possible world again, and only within it could she accept me. Our conversations never went below the level of the music, the classic poets, the mountainous great novels. She disdained anything below them with an uncompromising silence, waiting out the war in her way, as the grease-streaked girl by the radio was waiting it out in hers.

I only had five albums—the Brahms concerto, the Fauré Mass and two of the last quartets of Beethoven; the fifth had been given me as a going-away present when I left Washington. It was a rousing, martial, exotic group of songs sung by the Red Army chorus. Sometimes in the evening I sat in the library window letting it blare out, singing with it, all alone, "Pum pum pum,"—cavalry charges, Borodino, all the rest.

I also made new friends. One evening in the NAAFI, I sat at one of the beer-soaked tables waiting for my number to be called so I could gather my sausage and mash from the noisy NAAFI girl who never knew our names but bawled out our numbers as if she were at war with us all. An airman sat down beside me, or rather, slipped into the chair. I was a little surprised. After nearly a year I still had enough trouble with the language to make me stay to myself on evenings in the NAAFI. Only a few days before, I had gone up to a table and said, "Are you all through with the salt?" and backed away from the stunned silence of several airmen with their mouths full of sausage and mash. Finally, despairing, I had simply picked up the salt and retreated. "Through" in England does not mean "finished," as the GI's found when they fed coins into the public telephones and then were told by the operator that they were "through" when they hadn't even started to talk. They would hang up and retire in frustrated disgust while small boys waited to run in the booths, push button B and gather up change like playing the slot machine as soon as the GI's left.

So I waited for the airman to speak first.

"I've been wanting to talk to you," he said and glanced behind him. The gesture reminded me of a movie—I couldn't remember which one—that quick glance, only a twitch. He lounged back in his seat. I liked his looks. He had a bright, shrewd face, a sort of innocent snappiness, the speedy voice of a quick answer. That, too, seemed familiar.

Just then, in a bald, obscene yell, the bullish NAAFI girl called out my number.

"God, what a horror that woman is," he said.

I brought my sausage and mash back to the table. In this pale tan dish, in wartime, all the Puritan austerity of years of British cooking had been satisfied. It tasted of nothing, lying half submerged in some kind of ersatz gravy. When you poured catsup in it, it was like eating the wet brown paper the meat had once been wrapped in.

Behind me the woman bellowed again.

"She's all right, she's got a job to do." I defended her, ashamed of being so disgusted with her myself. "She's probably had to yell her way through life . . ."

"That's the trouble with you bourgeois converts," he fumed. "You just bring your snobbery with you. That woman would be a loud-mouthed bitch wherever she was."

I didn't understand what I'd been converted to, certainly not to sausage and mash.

"There are several of us here," he lowered his voice, sounding reverent. I couldn't see the smart face as a religious convert. "We'd like to talk with you. I always pride myself that I can pick out another person who thinks as I do. When I was in Fleet Street . . ."

I knew what kind of movie it had been from his way of sitting, his pub-level authority, his scanning of the room as if he were outside it, reading it, too aloof to be involved, his ease of taking possession of my attitudes; only his dress was wrong. He should have worn the dirty mackintosh, the snapbrim hat of a Fleet Street reporter—a very young Fleet Street reporter before the casual clothes slipped imperceptively from dash to scruff, before he realized that he in a tie slightly splattered with beer, was stuck and stunned, automatically turning out for too little pay and too little pride the half-dead clichéd prose of English run-of-mill journalism.

But LAC Horn was at the beginning of his career. He still, lounging in his Air Force uniform, had the innocent glamour.

"What'll you have?" he said, the authentic pub invitation. The NAAFI faded away from us.

"A half of bitter."

It was all the same, the dim, warm, watery NAAFI

beer. I couldn't tell the difference between mild and bitter, but I said the right words.

When he came back, he brought two other airmen, one with an intelligent, hard-working face, tough and stern. The other was a long, loose-jointed, loose-mouthed medical orderly I had seen running the MO's office when I had reported with a cold.

He had sat me down at a table, put a towel over my head and stuck a kettle of medicated vapor under my nose. Every time I had started to raise my head out of the tent to clear my eyes of the stinging steam, he had put his hand on my crown and said, "Not yet, luv," until I was steaming with sweat and vapor. Strangely enough, it had cured the racking cough.

" 'Ow's your cold, luv?" he asked and dropped himself and his pint down at the table.

We started exchanging those questions and answers of NAAFI conversation to be got out of the way quickly, but as necessary as ceremony. In peacetime, the medical orderly had been a day laborer, but he had been "going to be" a journalist, too. He had a curious pat language of ease that spattered off his tongue— "working-class solidarity," "the Hegelian Triad," "deviation." I began to see a very strong light.

The other said he was from Oxford.

"Look at her," LAC Horn laughed. "She thinks you're a bloody don! *You've* got a long way to go."

"Don't put her in a bind. She's on the right side. No, I'm at the Morris works, luv. A working man. That's more than I can say for you clots."

They forgot me, beginning an easy argument about whether the trade-union system was obsolete. I began to sort them out—the intellectual left wing of the station—the LAC and the medical orderly were Communists in their different ways: the Fleet Street LAC, class-conscious, smart, unemotional; the medical orderly, dedicated, converted, emotional, secondhand, loose and sad—a clinging belonger. In any organization— Communist, Fascist or religious—they would both have been dogs' bodies, one festering at his unrecognized worth in time, the other wagging his lonely tail. The man from the Morris works was a dedicated trade-union Socialist. Inner left-wing argument was complicated, and they seemed to swim easily in their differences, understanding what they meant, while I floundered.

"Why, I was taking political action when you clots were still crying for your mothers. The '26 strike—I was ten years old, throwing rotten tomatoes at the nobs running the trams. Bloody Oxford undergraduates turning it into one of their rags while the unemployed miners lay down in front of the Savoy." It sounded like part of a speech. "All you've ever done was pass out pamphlets."

The medical orderly began to dream. "I got knocked out in a fight with Mosley's Blackshirts when I was fifteen." He unwound himself from the back of his chair and looped his body over the table. "Now you," he said to me, "I know your lot. You haven't done a bloody thing. But you're with us, whether you know it or not. You just need educating—all you ex-bourgeoisie do. I'll lend you some books."

The trade-union man laughed. "God, more bloody pamphlets."

"We have something to go on when the emotions are ready."

"There you go, trusting emotions! That's the trouble with you . . ."

They veered away from me again, at it hammer and tongs.

"All you have to do is recognize the inevitability of the future . . ." the loose mouth of the medical orderly was like that of a man saying his catechism, using, one after another, in progression, a series of phrases he had learned as dogma; he began to shout, getting redder and redder, while LAC Horn went on watching, amused, and the trade-union man from Oxford flipped him back and forth, sparring easily.

At any moment I expected the medical orderly to crown his cause by saying a thundering "Jesus says so."

I had finally remembered where I had heard that kind of passion before—the undigested phrases, the dedication, the unquestioning blind stability that was only frozen, never to be changed by logic. He was like a small-town American religious convert who had "come to Jesus" and had his life changed overnight. He was nearly crying, as the other two, amused, manipulated him, LAC Horn staying just on his side, but enjoying the whole thing too much to be his defender.

"*She* knows." The medical orderly finally turned to me for help. "*She plays the Red Army chorus.*"

I knew why they had sought me out.

Afterward I had two listeners to the music. The red-haired girl would leave when the classics had been played, over and over, until they rasped on the turntable. At a knock on the door, she would get up and go without a word, jarred out of her peace, too angry at the medical orderly to speak; and he would lounge in to hear the Red Army chorus, as rapt as she had been, taking me into his world, ignoring any other.

At first he had me fooled. I didn't realize that when he talked about Eisenstein he wasn't talking about his art. He was seeing himself heroic, storming the Winter Palace, fighting the Teutonic Knights, as some small boys after going to Westerns practice the first draw. When he mentioned the milk-separator sequence, I thought he meant the milk-separator sequence—its sexuality, its form—but he didn't. He had no taste, only passion, and he used it all in a faraway love affair with the steppes. There was no more use in arguing with him than with someone in a hypnotic trance. He stayed in it. Somewhere out there, there was an ideal Russia, and he was part of it, no longer an ungainly medical orderly with a duty-worn collar and bitten-bloody fingernails. He would lean against the wall, hearing not the record but the soldiers, his face guileless with relief.

One Tuesday, he met me when I came off duty at four o'clock. He was excited.

"I've told them about you. They say you can come to the meeting tonight," he told me, proud of himself.

"What meeting?"

He looked around the empty tarmac as if the whole of British Intelligence were waiting to close in.

"The cell in Combe Whitley."

I wanted to laugh. Combe Whitley was a fairly grimy village about eight miles from the station, that most of us avoided because it had a small glue factory that made the air smell and polluted the water of the narrow stream. Even the industrial waste that had ruined the village and that hung in the heavy air had a sad droop about it, as if it couldn't hope to succeed in making even the first inroads of a black belt. It just filtered and wafted unpleasantly through the village trees.

I must have been smiling, because he looked as hurt as if I'd laughed aloud at him.

"Oh never mind, if you don't care about it. I just thought you would." He was turning away. If recruiting to the party had depended on members like him, so easily hurt, I could never see it spreading into a dangerous minority in England.

"I'd like to go," I said to his back.

At once that guileless look of pleasure chased the sulking away from his face.

"You won't regret it," he said seriously.

I was interested and excited, cycling up the evening road toward the smell of Combe Whitley. By the time we were ready to meet at the gate, I had recruited my dependable guides to go with us. Perhaps I expected them to guide me through English politics in their dirrerent ways, as they guided me past the haunted tree. The medical orderly was annoyed and, I thought, a little nervous at the prospect of taking an officer along, too. But by the time we had gone a mile from the station he and the civilian librarian were engulfed in a private abstract argument to the point of ignoring us. The pilot was calling me a bloody fool. The lay preacher cycled along behind us, enjoying the evening, ignoring us all. We rode on, an ill-assorted group, to anyone passing, solidity of Air-Force-blue, toward the Communist meeting.

The evening breeze was blowing in our direction. The bicycles dragged against it, and the smell of burned hair and garbage reached us across the evening long before we rode across the little bridge. There was no square, no manor house—Combe Whitley must have begun as a huddle of houses around a ford, because the stone bridge we crossed was at the center of the village. Upstream, the small glue factory drooped along the bank. The water running under the bridge was brown; dirty, fawn-colored foam lapped at the weeds along the bank.

We dismounted in front of the Queen's Head.

"A singularly fine place for the revolution to begin," the pilot whispered.

"Oh shut up," I muttered back. He was embarrassing me. But I walked into the pub suppressing a giggle.

The inevitable old men in the public bar didn't bother to look around when we filed through to the saloon. The medical orderly tapped lightly on the door and made a show of listening. Someone inside opened the door a fraction, closed it while we waited outside, then opened it a little wider to let each of us file in.

Outside it was a fine fall day. Inside the saloon they had managed a sad little atmosphere of secrecy. The fire was lit but refused to do anything but add a smell of dirty coal to the smell from the glue factory that had permeated the room for so long. A large beat-up table stood in the center under a dull dining-room light. It was the only light. It touched faintly the dark brown walls and the dirty pub painting of a canal in Venice with the faint outline left of a gondola. The rest of the room was in darkness. I could see vague figures in the gloom. There had been six people in the room, so when we came in we filled it, jarred the mood, scraped chairs, glanced at each other, finally settled into the meeting and let the atmosphere catch and smoulder.

I remember clasped hands lying around the table under the Electrolier, the droning solemn voices, the old brown linoleum on the floor. I realized what it was that seemed so known already: the tensile closeness, the rhetorical rise and fall of a man's speech. I had once been taken to Wednesday-night meeting in the same king of Puritan living room by my grandmother. Only the language had changed; the feeling of conversion, of belonging, of having a secret answer to cling to was exactly the same.

The man in the cap was droning on about the terrible conditions in the factory as if it were some great plant in the Midlands with a dark sea of workmen on bicycles coming off shift in the evening light. He spoke of it all as if he had made his speech a thousand times before— even the professional shifting of his voice, stirring up the little room, sounded to me as if his thoughts were someplace else. In the background a woman kept breathing out the words "strike, strike" like people murmuring, "yes," and "Amen, brother," at a sermon.

The central talk came to a halt and there was a silence, a waiting for the spirit to move someone. Then a man cleared his throat. "Open the second front now," he said.

"George, you old fool, don't you hear the news? We've landed in Italy." The woman who had been murmuring "strike" reached forward out of the dark and hit him on the shoulder. George subsided, humiliated.

The medical orderly, happy in his element, had left us all behind. He lounged so far back in his chair that his face was in darkness; only his long lanky body showed in the light. "In my opinion," he said slowly, "they are only doing this as a gesture, because we've demanded it. It's not enoof."

Italy had surrendered a few days before.

It was funny, but I found myself trying to keep from crying at the pathetic security of the dedicated, cut-off flotsam in the room.

After the meeting, we had beer while one by one the members bundled themselves up against an alien world and sidled through the door singly so that no one would know there had been a meeting. The old men didn't bother to look up as we passed by them.

On the way home, even the pilot was quiet. We had

all caught the sadness—even, for once, the medical orderly, who had no more to say, but rode along a little apart from the rest of us, his head down, looking, in the near darkness, like the head of an old turtle.

I asked him once if he had met the Russian at the station, the amorous sergeant.

He hung his head in that turtle way.

"I don't think he's a party member," he said, "he couldn't talk about anything."

LAC Horn had been there when they met.

"Did you ever hear a Slav laugh?" was all he said about it.

Those two, jostled together by their conversion, formed a close dislike for each other, a party split between them. LAC Horn was what I would learn to recognize as one of the "intellectual" minority—his taste was as orthodox in its way as the medical orderly's. LAC Horn read *The Week,* the medical orderly read *The Daily Worker;* LAC Horn cared only for erudite jazz—Django Reinhardt was his God; he sang "When I First Met Lucille" to himself in the NAAFI, the medical orderly yearned over my records. LAC Horn thought the *Colossus of Maroussi* the finest book of the twentieth century. On leave in London, he was killed by a V-1, the pattern of his future already assumed, his change and sway. He had no time to become, at forty, an angry young man.

One day a messenger came into the flying control room when I was on duty.

"You're to report to the CO as soon as you come off duty," he ordered.

"Why?" I asked.

"Orders."

He walked out.

I sat for the rest of my watch in freezing fear. King's Regulations is a thick book. A few looks into it can convince any other rank that anything she might dream of doing for natural everyday survival has been forbidden someplace in its rules. It was possible only to slide through the maze of orders, do one's best and, for the rest, hope to live without getting caught. By the time my watch was over, I had committed every crime in the book. But I did think, pathetically, that my crimes were too unimportant to interest that faraway, aloof and splendid-moustached commanding officer of the large station, whom I had spoken to only once, on the parade ground, standing to a rigid attention and staring past his head while he ordered me to go to the American Red Cross canteen in Bath. Since then he had never looked my way, even when he returned my salutes as we passed each other; my head would snap toward him, but his movements of head and hand were casual and easy, his salute a gentleman's gesture, mine rigid from drill.

I was marched into his office, resolved to plead guilty and throw myself at his mercy.

"At ease," he said without looking at me. He was looking harassed, holding a telephone to his head, staring beyond it out of the office window.

"I said *vodka,*" he ordered into it, annoyed, and hung up.

"Why they have to put this off onto me," he told me. "I don't know what to do." He looked plaintive.

"Sir," I answered, the frozen "at ease" hurting my behind.

"I've heard your records," he said, "they sounded lovely. I've often wanted to come up and listen, but I was afraid I wouldn't be welcome. Oh don't stand like that. It makes me nervous."

I relaxed my behind.

"We're in an absolutely ghastly mess," he went on. "I have to entertain two bloody Russian officers for an inspection. I've got all the food and drink. It was damn hard to get. I've been on the scrounge all over Group. But what the devil are we going to talk about? I suppose they'll bring an interpreter—do you think? Would you mind? I mean I'm frightfully sorry I can't ask you to join us, but there won't be any other ranks at the . . ." He was highly embarrassed. "I thought. There's a small balcony in the mess hall. Do you think you might . . . sort of stay up there through the thing . . . and bring your records of the Red Army singers?" He suddenly smiled. "Don't you think it would be wizard?"

"Sir," I said.

"Oh stop that"—he was petulant—"talk to me about it. I'm in an awful bind."

On the day of the inspection the station had its greatest cleanup for a year.

There was much discussion among the officers about where the hammer-and-sickle flag should be flown. Finally it was draped across the balcony, where I was to crouch, hidden behind it, with the library phonograph and the Red Army records. From the way the rumors were flying, I think they expected two cossacks to ride whooping onto the station on their steppe ponies with snow on their boots.

At 1900 hours, the CO's car called for me at the library, and I, the records and the phonograph were delivered to the small dim balcony high on the wall above the tables of the officer's mess. The light through the red flag made the alcove into a little, infrared room. Far away in the distance I could hear the buzz of officers having drinks. The orderly who got me settled and hidden in the balcony told me that it was going well.

"They've been boozing in there since seventeen hundred," he said bitterly. He sounded bitter about almost everything.

We made a peephole for me under the flag, and, flat on the floor, I watched the door with one hand outstretched to set the record going. The machine was on, the volume high.

At 2000 hours, eight o'clock, the double doors to the mess were flung open and I turned on the music. In the little enclosed room it was deafening.

The CO marched in, grinning, with a small happy Russian on each arm, their boots gleaming, all their faces wreathed happily in vodka. The Russians began to slap at each other across the tall Englishman's chest, delighted with the music.

The noise in the room was a dim roar. The Red

Army chorus raced among the clatter of plates and silver. On the second record, one of the Russians leaned across the CO again, banged on the table and, joined by the other, burst into song. I suppose I was playing a Russian counterpart of "Roll Out the Barrel." The CO looked up toward the red flag and made a V-for-Victory signal. When they had finished, there was much applause.

The bitter mess attendant crawled over beside me with a glass of water and a plate of food. I took a drink. It wasn't water. The CO had sent me vodka. I put on another record. As the party grew noisier, the vodka kept arriving in the balcony. Flat on the floor, changing records, drinking vodka, I went on and on, eye to the peephole, no time passing. Some time later the party was over. The bitter orderly bundled what was left of me, the records and the phonograph into the CO's car and we were delivered back to the library.

The next day the CO called me in to thank me. He was beaming.

"Your Communist records were an enormous success," he told me. "The Russians would say 'that reminds me' and the interpreter would translate revolutionary stories while they smiled. It was most interesting. I'm glad they're gone. Oh dear." He did look hung over.

I went on standing at ease, waiting to be dismissed.

"I've been wanting to say . . ." His embarrassment was more painful than his hangover. "We wanted to say . . . your coming over and all. Very fine. Uh, is it difficult?"

"Sometimes, sir."

"What I wanted to say . . . Don't take any nonsense from anyone . . . below the rank of sergeant . . . Uh, dismissed."

I went straight to the library, packed up the album and took it to the medical orderly. "Here," I told him, "are some Communist records for you. I can't stand them anymore."

He was very pleased and wanted to talk.

"Do you really think," he began, leaning against the sick-bay wall, "that the end justifies the means?"

"Frankly, no," I said and walked out.

The next time I listened to my music, I played the Fauré Mass again. I felt safe and alone. The red-haired girl, who also had decided I was Communist because of the Red Army records, had gone off to sulk. I knew I could listen for once without starting anybody's world turning in my orbit, taking part of me for granted as part of them.

There was a knock at the door. I grumbled, "Come in."

It was the Catholic padré, a Jesuit priest.

"I wonder if I might come in," he said. "I hear you're listening to the Fauré Mass. Of course, as you know, we aren't officially allowed to use modern Masses, but it is so beautiful, I would . . ."

"Come in and sit down, sir," I told him, "but I think you ought to know at once, *I'm not Catholic* and I don't believe that the end justifies the means."

"That may be so," he said, the pleasure of a polemic exercise showing in his voice as he relaxed—I had forgotten that Jesuits are the most difficult people in the world to argue with, and I did only want to listen to the music.

As soon as the Mass was over, he said, like a hungry man, "Yes, what you say may be so in some circumstances. However . . ."

Chapter 10

But outside of the secret and accidental connections, a sort of stumbling together through taste or individual circumstance, the taboos between groups on such a large station were unbridgeable gulfs, to be crossed only in times of crisis and with great force. These crossings were punishable. The isolation between the ranks was traditional. To break it was to suffer. Sometimes this punishment took on all the methods of a small, organized martyrdom against which there was no built-in protection in the wingless parts of the Air Force, as there was in the Army and the Navy.

There were eight of us on a train, and one soldier in full kit. He sat and listened to us complain—not about ill-treatment necessarily, but about a sense of wrong we could not put into words, could only blast about in ineffectual stories which sounded too unimportant to tell; it is hard to make a plot of indifference. He said, "Our efforts would never treat us like that. They've got to go into action with us—and we have this." He patted his rifle.

We, too, had a weapon—silence—and all too seldom a kind of solidarity of despair or anger that could shoot up through the other groups, as isolated from each other as we from them in the military hierarchy. Sometimes it was done individually.

Viv did it through sturdy innocence. During the year between initial training and her posting to Turnbull St. Justin, she had been in a small, proud, independent balloon barrage unit. She had gone through the hard, concentrated discipline of training, but she had never faced the debilitating discipline of isolation, boredom and neglect, within which we made our small, fiercely protected worlds on the station. We suffered more often from the attrition of threats of unnamed punishments, meted out in secret, unknown to the officers, than we did from direct contact with power. It was the secret threats that taught us the patience of fear.

Viv would have none of it. For some weeks before she came, the airwomen's mess had suffered in charge of our food one of those obscene, loud-mouthed, filthy men; whose small power had grown in the cookhouse until he ruled as a tsar in a food-streaked apron over the few frightened cookhouse girls who could not fight back because he was a corporal. In their jobs he was the only NCO they came into daily contact with. They fought him only by neglecting the food, so that their lowered morale seemed to poison it. It was thrown into our plates as we held them out over the steaming cauldrons of swill which were set on a serving table beside two open garbage bins. When we had finished eating, we took our plates back and scraped them into the bins. By the time the mess had been open half an hour, the smell of the thrown garbage had mingled with the smell from the cauldrons to form a thick, scummy miasma over the mess.

One day the stew was actually sour. Girl after girl, not daring to speak, brought it back untouched and scraped it back into the garbage under the satisfied smile of the fat corporal, who, because he had to work in the heat of the cauldrons, wore his filthy cookhouse apron over a pair of once-white overalls; he had a naked look about him.

That day, as Viv and I sat down with out plates, a neat, pert little WAAF officer came in and marched from table to table in a sort of formal, blind inspection, stopping at each table to say, "Any complaints?"

We could hear her coming through the silence. She stood at the end of the table.

"Any complaints?" I heard her say, bored, above my head, bowed like all the others, into my sour-smelling plate.

I felt Viv get up. There was a little gasp from the other women and then a deeper silence.

"Airwoman!" the little WAAF officer said.

"Smell it, ma'am," Viv said and sat down.

The officer seemed, for the first time, to realize where she was. She did make a close inspection of the food, the filth, and as she started to leave she stopped again at the table.

"Thank you, Airwoman," she said to Viv's embarrassed head. "If you other girls would have the courage to speak out as she has done, we could do something." I thought she sounded a little lost.

When she had left, one of the women across the table looked at Viv. "You should have known better."

"This ain't fit to eat!" Viv turned the stew over on

her plate. "Why shouldn't we complain? That's wot they're for, in' it?"

"You'll find out," the WAAF told her.

She did. Viv had committed the unpardonable sin of going over the head of an NCO directly to an officer in a channel opened by King's Regulations but completely closed by tradition, which formed one of the strongest of the deep, unspoken barriers between officers and other ranks. It was formed by an agreed recognition of the need, within the hidden world of other ranks, to stick together against authority, the enemy, and it was perverted into a kind of silent dictatorship by ourselves, from not the destruction but the gradual erosion of dignity that can be caused by too long exposure to indifference and fear.

Like a disease, one could not know it was happening until the first warning signs appeared: a quickening of the heart, a closing of the facial expression to stone on being spoken to by an officer, a learning to take up as little space as possible, as if to be noticed were to bear a punishment in itself. Viv had been one of the lucky minority in active units small enough for names to be known instead of numbers; she had had the simple communal job to do of raising the barrage balloons. She had experienced no personal attrition, but rather, an expansion and acceptance she had not known before in her life. When she did face indifference, it came too quickly, and it did not quite "take" with her. Time had not robbed her of her freedom.

For a few days after the incident of the complaint, the mess was clean, the food was better, the corporal even changed his apron. Then circumstances, as if they were too heavy to be shored up so late and in such a tired time, collapsed back to normal; the corporal's apron collected new stains day after day, the food went back to its combined smell of dead animals and tannic acid. All went along as before, and from time to time the officers marched through it chanting, "Any complaints? Any complaints?" like a litany with no response.

Through it all, the return to normal, Viv took her punishment. She got nothing to eat. We were not allowed to touch the ladles in the food. We held out our plates to have it dumped on them in assembly line as we moved from vat to vat. Viv's plate was ignored. The other girls at the table would share with her when they weren't being watched by the corporal, but our rations were small—two-thirds that of the men—and Viv's strong muscular body needed as much food as any of the men on the station.

Anger, a sense of injustice, turn inward at the punishment of "being sent to Coventry." Viv could not answer. She only moved within a worrying silence, ate in the NAAFI when she got paid and waited—and presented her plate at every meal.

On the tenth day, Viv's plate was filled. The punishment was over, the unspoken order given—not a word or a glance showed the change—just the flinging of the inevitable stew from the ladle. Her stomach, shrunk from the rationing anyway, then forced to fast, could not take it. She ate a few bites, then waited for me, and together we took our plates up to dump the remains into the open garbage bins.

The fat corporal had watched her all through dinner. He stood waiting in front of the bins. When Viv's hands went forward over the bins to scrape her plate, he reached forward and grabbed her wrist.

"No you don't," he told her. "Eat it."

"Not bloody likely," Viv answered, watching his fingers around her wrist. She let the food, plate and all, fall into the swill.

"We'll see about this," I heard the corporal mutter. He turned away from her.

Viv's foot came up and caught him in the seat of his dirty overalls. His arms went wide, but there was nothing to catch at but the steaming air. He went spreadeagle into the bins—garbage and corporal were splayed over the floor.

"You struck an NCO. You'll get a court martial." He was trying to pick himself up off the slick floor.

"Not likely." Viv looked down at him, not bothering to smile at the sight. "King's Regulations. Don't lay hands on an other rank." She added happily, "I 'ad to defend meself."

She never heard officially of the incident again, but her action, for a few days, cleared the air. The voices of the WAAF were heard in the mess, calling across the tables with a new ease.

Morale was so delicate, so barometerlike in its exposure to circumstance, that an incident like this could make it shoot up. We gathered courage from each other. One action was done for us all, one injustice depleted us again. Just as delicately, morale could slip and lower—a bad officer, an unjust or blind action, a death in flying threatened us all.

Coming back off leave a month later I sensed, as I signed in, that lowering of temperature, the silence of one of those barometric tumbles so subtly caused that often no one could say what it was, how it had started. We could only suffer it until the temperature changed again. Being American—more frenetic, more anarchic by the training of my past to the quick violence of stepping forward, to what we like to think of as initiative—I had a heightened sense of such a lowered atmosphere. It made me impatient to the point of feeling trapped at the quiet, almost bucolic patience of the people around me. It seemed negative, dead. I was wrong. It was only a different way of action. It even had a name, the silent mutiny of the British other ranks. It was called dumb insolence. At the time, signing in that evening, I only registered the silence.

At the billet Viv told me that there was a new WAAF commanding officer on the station and that, at the last inspection, she had insisted that the coal in the coal bins be washed piece by piece. There needed be no more facts about the woman. The brutality that sticks in one's craw forever is not that of quick passion or even of active cruelty, perhaps because the sane are, themselves, capable at some time of such action and therefore understand it. The brutality that diminishes is that of circumstance, of the insane moments of obedience to folly simply because folly has power—the perfect absurdity of following form when the sane substance is at odds with it. Looking back, I can forgive and understand being attacked by the women and thrown down the stairs, but I can never reconcile my own cowardice, my own state of diminished pride, in which I followed a sergeant on her bicycle, running along behind her, simply because I was ordered to. To Viv and to the others who had done it, the turning point, the obscenity, had been the washing of the coal in the bins.

After it the new WAAF CO, a tall, awkward woman with a heavy chin and sullen, beaten eyes, walked through corridors of silence. To counteract it, she tightened discipline, as if the one protection the women had was subject to command.

Two days later she instituted WAAF pack drill as a punishment. The order broke what morale was left on the station, affecting us all, at the same time connecting us all like the lines of breakage starred out on glass.

WAAF pack drill differed from the pack drill for the men in one respect. Our full kit was lighter. We had no arms. We wore for it packs, helmets and gas equipment, and we marched on punishment at the double, alone, before the yelled commands of a sergeant, around the otherwise empty parade ground in full view of the whole station. There was little physical brutality in the punishment, but the English are fairly used to corporal punishment. They are slapped as children if they are working class and beaten if they are "educated." The one Anglo-Saxon torture which goes beyond physical brutality is humiliation. For a nation whose deepest emotion is embarrassment, it is almost unbearable. The first WAAF given the punishment deserted.

The second girl received the punishment for coming back two hours late off leave. She appeared behind the sergeant, her head hanging, her kit strapped on, at 1700 hours. It was usually an active, busy time around the parade ground. Airmen and women were crowding the doors of the mess and the NAAFI on one side of the square. The sergeant's mess on the left side of the square was full of noise, and on the other side, at the airmen's barracks, men leaned out to call to each other from the windows. The blare of the Light Program came from the buildings, its sound permeating the atmosphere at tea-time.

On that day, two hours before blackout time, without, so far as I could tell, a single word being said, every blackout curtain that abutted the parade ground was drawn—in the mess, the sergeant's mess, the barracks windows. There was not a soul to be seen. The station had a dead, waiting silence about it. I saw, only by glance, the WAAF, tiny on the huge square, and heard, far away, the faint voice of the sergeant drilling her, and, as the others did, I turned away quickly.

Three civilian workmen from the maintenance unit on the station, stopped beside the parade ground to see what was going on. I saw, in the distance, three men walk out of the sergeant's mess and take them by the arms. In dead silence, they moved along through the yellow evening mist to the barracks gate, their bodies slow and heavy.

There was no more WAAF pack drill. For a week after the incident the station rested in a kind of uneasy silence, waiting to see if the trouble was over. Women fought over trifles. Barracks cots were left unmade. People sat in the movies, dim, tired, without reaction. Having reached a dangerous, still point, it was taking time for the barometer to rise, for the station to come alive again. When it did, it exploded—but still in complete silence—mutinous, communal dumb insolence.

In the cold and brutal division between the officers and the other ranks, when morale was so low, both sides waited for an act, an almost chemical change; all were keyed to some direction to jump. Within the waiting we did our jobs, had a few more accidents, wrote letters, talked of other things, were wary. Then the word began to spread to break the tension and the silence.

An eighteen-year-old boy, a volunteer from Canada,

wrote home to his family. The mood of the station crept into the letter, one of those homesick pleas that must have gone out like little weak tendrils across the war-time gulf of circumstance over and over, to be read, and savored and misunderstood. He told, because there were no words to put the atmosphere of the station into, of a mild sickness—the sickness we all had from time to time, of debilitation and disappointment; the feeling that the great personal decisions of the young in that tired time were doomed in the conscript world to attrition, to smallness, to the necessary cowardice of having to watch brutality without action, to take part in it without speaking, to diminish and shrink for survival. He mentioned the sight that finally sickened him: one lone WAAF girl in the yellow air, going through the ignominious punishment of pack drill.

The letter was censored. He was called before the worried station commander, whose command for weeks had been slipping away from him in the silence, who was panicking toward any action that would give him control again. I could sense, from that small contact I had had with him, that mild upper-class petulance turning into a real and dangerously undirectional anger capable of striking anywhere, because he was disturbed out of his habits and landed, floundering, beyond his capacity to understand. To the frightened Canadian airman, he was only his rank—air commodore—one of those heard-of ranks coming from some higher, faceless and charismatic world that most airmen never saw, except when they flicked past their attention-locked eyes at rare march-pasts. The boy, innocent, caught by such panic, was staggered at the thought of being in the same room with the man. A huge spotlight had been turned on him, almost by accident, powered by the unspoken quarrel, and he, pinned there, was too stunned to be clever, to burrow away from the light toward his own anonymity again.

He stood to attention on his first charge, a thin, neat boy with the bad complexion of a frustrated adolescent, his ears at right angles to his close-cropped mousy hair—an unknown boy who would turn into an unknown man. In front of the officer lay his letter home. He recognized his own schoolboy hand. He was told that he had lied—not in words, but in meaning—since the phrase "pack drill" was understood by civilians as a masculine punishment, which meant carrying a rifle.

The boy stood there, not understanding the manipulation of his letter, not even knowing it was serious, listening to the word-splitting absurdity, trying to sort it out. He said afterward that the air commodore had sounded "kindly" when he gave him his choice between accepting punishment or standing a court martial. The words "court martial" were a daily threat, a thing far away, to be feared as an unknown, a finality. The boy chose to accept punishment. As yet, he said, his "crime" had not been named.

He was given twenty-eight days at Chorley Detention Barracks for the crime of "spreading dissention in a major dominion." The dumb insolence had been broken, the victim found, martyred by both sides to precipitate action and break the silence none of us could stand.

Dumb insolence shifted toward mutiny. While the boy was waiting to be sent to Chorley, he was kept under close arrest and marched to meals—a slight, frail figure flanked by four MP's. We rode by him on our bicycles, an anonymous flow of other ranks, and called out messages—impotent and active. He still looked stunned, his eyes straight forward, as if, having learned that to move was to be noticed and punished, he never wanted to move again.

If the phrase "court martial" struck awe in other ranks and the rank of air commodore conjured an unknown power and magic, the word "Chorley" struck pure terror. It was known only by rumor, by threat. Chorley was the word for hell. I had only known one person who had been "in Chorley." It was the conscientious objector—but he, after three sentences there, still retained his saintly self-hypnosis about the world. He said it was bad, but added that there was good there as every place, if you looked for it. He was of little use in finding out what it was like.

One day I, in the security of being too low in the scheme of things to fall any farther, stopped a wing commander I knew and asked him if the officers could do anything to intercede for the boy. He looked shocked.

"I'm only a wing commander. What could I do?" he asked me, defeated before he could think of action. In him, as in all of us, was the learned irresponsibility of acquiescence to authority—as if there were no master but abstract authority itself. I saw the hierarchy as like peeling an onion, skin after skin, with no end except the military mind itself, seeking its master at whatever rank. Like the onion, when it was peeled away, nothing was there but an abstraction—a "they."

Those who were unquestioning wore it as their own, until in flashes, like the wing commander standing there uncertain on the tarmac, they saw it outside themselves and cringed and turned from it, diminished as the rest. I have wondered since what the air commodore feared that made him shift the blame for that haunting insolence he could not control onto such a mild young airman and send him off to Chorley for such a little crime.

The rebellion, pushed to the point of exhaustion, flattened into dead calm, filtered away, died down. We had, for a little while, drawn together in our anger, thrown ourselves against the facts of wartime military life we could not change, but only be caught and shrunk by.

When the boy came back from Chorley a few weeks later, he had lost eighteen pounds. He said nothing, and after a few embarrassed days of sympathy, we let him sink back, forgotten. Our capacity for rebellion melted away, for who can be rebelled against when everyone has a master and when, if we had really talked about what we hated and put it into words, we would have found only agreement? There were, when the calm returned, changes, slowly made, reverberating back to us.

The WAAF CO who had begun it was posted. The barometer of morale began gradually to rise again.

Whether the young boy had to do with it, I don't know, but some time later, there was an inquiry into the running of Chorley. The conscientious objector was called to give evidence. He saw it all as another of his daily blessings because it gave him two days' leave.

What other psychic scars were caused I don't know. How can we tell? Did we draw together a little more? Did we learn to care a little less? Was it forgotten, shrugged away by the others? We got out our knitting, got on with the mechanics of our jobs, settled again to waiting through the gray days, went on pass to the cold bedrooms of wartime boarding houses, sat together under the faint blue lights of blacked-out trains moving through months of damp winter and night, forgot the Canadian boy's name. Bigger injustices happened; there was more blood, more absurd death in other places.

But the value of an action is exactly that—its value, its opening of possibility, its tearing away of protective illusion. After the incident it was too late for me to deny the possibilities of where I was, the recognition that I was trapped among the thousands within a system where, if we were protected from the cruder psychopathic actions (and often not from those—authority, let loose, finds its own excuses), we were exposed naked to the illogical flicks of the human mind that forced us into diminishing situations, anonymity, debility of soul. The awareness of being at the mercy of such caprice was boglike in its uncertain threat. Authority, to the anonymous, had long arms but no discernible, respected head. What strength I found, I found in the surviving underground, among my friends.

Two weeks after the boy came back from Chorley, I had my first evidence of "signals shock," the experience of a revolt of my aural sense, the inefficiency of brain. Into the enemy jamming which, by now, was never out of my waking mind, fake messages began to intrude, as they had to my watch mate when she was asleep. The messages drifted over from dreams to the edge of my hearing, to the watch itself, and in the night, lulled by the hours before morning, in the trancelike waiting, I would suddenly hear calls for help out of the night ether, "Hello, Darky. Hello, Darky," and I would clutch the set to tune in aural visions—nothing there but the night and my own anxiety for action.

It was a classic disintegration, once it began. On a bus, coming back from a day pass at Bath, I sat watching the dark fields slip by, relaxed into exposure. Suddenly I got the bends, a revolt of my gut. Walking like an old woman, clutching my distended stomach, I had to be helped from the bus to the sick bay by Viv, finding, finally, the safety of a bed, the protection of collapse. I lay awake all night, listening to the phantom calls come in as if I were tuned to trouble from the airborne lost all over England.

In the morning, a young MO examined me, already knowing what he would have to say. In the evening he came back and sat cross-legged on the end of my cot, like a small boy, relaxed for a little while from duty.

"You weighed ten stone when you joined up. Now you weigh eight." He was looking at the wall, not at me. I tried to translate to myself—140 pounds to 112 pounds. I hadn't known it. His mind wandered over what he could do with me. "Do you know anyone in London?" he finally asked.

I said I did.

"I'm going to give you a week's sick leave, starting tomorrow. Go into London and find a job and get a transfer out."

I was too weak. I started to cry. Somehow, with all the wrong of it, I didn't want to leave them. The troubles were abstract; my friends were real. For the first time in my life I had known the underworld—the saving, miraculous individuality of the great, moving mass we live in that survives while the privileged, thinking they guide and rule, sport themselves like a school of high fish around the whale's mouth. In the wrong place and at the wrong time, I had met the common negative experience of ten-tenths of the world—indifference. In a more responsible, romantic job I would never have known it. I would have been fulfilled by the insidious satisfaction of action, would, like so many, have carried from the war only nostalgia, no wound. I would have had no reason, twenty years later, to open the wound for the unknown other ranks to write this book, to tell about the gray, forgotten mass that suffer the state of war.

I lay on the cot and cried, while the MO, not understanding, thought it was only weakness and fatigue and tried, in his annoyed Anglo-Saxon embarrassment at tears, to comfort me.

"You're bloody lucky," he said. "I wish I could work my ticket. I'm browned off."

Two weeks later, I was being driven to the station in the back of an RAF van. In civilian clothes that no longer fitted, with a one-way pass to London, three pounds ten and my "ticket"—my discharge—in my pocket, I was on the way to the American Office of War Information in London, the cocktail parties, the conferences, the PX cigarettes, the frenetic turmoil of people who had names and thought they were running the juggernaut of war, which was only spending itself toward its own death like a great tiring unled beast.

As the van turned out of the gate of RAF Turnbull St. Justin, I saw Viv, standing in front of the guardhouse. Her cap was as jaunty as ever behind the high pompadour, her battle dress grease covered. Tears streaked her dirty face and my new civilian makeup.

"Ah, you dirty civie," she called out. "Get some in."

I never saw any of them again.